Attending to the spiritual restlessness of humanity that manifests in migration/immigration, Dr. Hosffman Ospino addresses the relational encounter through culture that is required of the church. The resounding reminder that God always encounters through culture, in ethnic, sociological, and historical contexts, is inspirational for catechesis today.

👋 MARGARET MATIJASEVIC, *Executive Director,*
National Conference for Catechetical Leadership

D1360534

One of the most innovative pastoral theologians in our country provides us with practical wisdom addressing the most urgent questions about being Catholic in our diverse U.S. communities. If you seek an accessible yet profound understanding of catechesis in a multicultural church, this is the resource for you!

👋 TIMOTHY MATOVINA, *author of **Latino Catholicism:***
Transformation in America's Largest Church

A timely and invaluable resource! In bringing together theory, research, and practice, Dr. Ospino has provided a practical resource for catechists seeking to understand the importance of language and culture in the process of faith formation and its transmission.

👋 JAVIER W. BUSTAMANTE, *Executive Director of the Office*
of Cultural Diversity and Outreach in the Archdiocese of Washington

Hosffman presents a practical, inspiring, and engaging book for all parish leaders committed to religious education and evangelization. It captures the current fundamental experience of life, faith, and culture.

👋 REV. LUIS A. GUIDO, *artist and poet, author of **Amar con Sabiduría***
es Saber Volar

Just when the felt need is so acute, along comes Ospino with an excellent comprehensive work on the encounter between faith and culture within the context of catechesis. A valuable resource for catechists and church leaders in their efforts to respond to the call of the gospel in a culturally diverse society.

👋 SR. RUTH BOLARTE, IHM, D.MIN., *Director, Office of Multi-Cultural*
Ministry, Diocese of Metuchen

Cultural diversity is the reality today in the American Catholic Church: it is not a goal or an option! Hosffman Ospino leads catechists gently and concretely through this current reality to a deeper consciousness and appreciation of the relationship between faith and culture. While demonstrating this relationship through the writings of the church, he gives practical "dos" and "don'ts" for catechesis in U.S. Catholic churches and dioceses.

❧ **BARBARA ROMANELLO-WICHTMAN, D.MIN.,** *Director of Religious Education and Catechesis for the Diocese of Columbus, Ohio*

Professor Ospino has presented an important pedagogical approach to effectively sharing the faith in a culturally diverse church and community. This is a must-have guide packed with practical tools and tips for catechists and catechetical leaders that will assist us in the art of sharing the faith within the complexity of our culturally diverse contexts.

❧ **PETER J DUCTRÁM, MA., M.DIV.,** *Archdiocesan Director of Catechesis, Archdiocese of Miami; member of the Federation for Catechesis with Hispanics NCCL*

An indispensable tool for today's catechist! Ospino provides a great summary of the church's wisdom on why culture matters, and he provides excellent, experience-tested tips for religious educators.

❧ **MAR MUÑOZ-VISOSO, MTS,** *Executive Director, Cultural Diversity in the Church, United States Conference of Catholic Bishops*

This essential guide responds to the needs that catechists face today. Dr. Ospino, using direct, clear, and concrete language, enumerates the challenges and offers recommendations for responding to them. This is an excellent pastoral resource for catechists.

❧ **REV. ALEJANDRO LÓPEZ-CARDINALE,** *President, The National Catholic Network de Pastoral Juvenil Hispana*

The ESSENTIAL CATECHIST'S BOOKSHELF

Interculturalism *and* Catechesis

A CATECHIST'S GUIDE
TO RESPONDING TO
CULTURAL DIVERSITY

Hosffman Ospino, Ph.D.

TWENTY-THIRD
PUBLICATIONS
twentythirdpublications.com

Dedication

To my dear friend María Pilar Latorre.

Thanks for your passionate dedication to catechesis,

your friendship, love, and inspiration.

Much of your wisdom is in the pages of this book.

TWENTY-THIRD PUBLICATIONS
1 Montauk Avenue, Suite 200, New London, CT 06320
(860) 437-3012 » (800) 321-0411 » www.twentythirdpublications.com

COVER PHOTO: ISTOCKPHOTO.COM/FATCAMERA

ISBN: 978-1-62785-260-9
Library of Congress Catalog Card Number: 2017932942
Printed in the U.S.A.

Contents

INTRODUCTION

What a wonderful time to be a Catholic catechist in the United States of America! My hope is that you agree. I am sure that many other catechists said something similar thirty, fifty, one hundred, and more years ago. Most likely they were right. Announcing the Good News of Jesus Christ and the richness of the Christian tradition is a great reason to rejoice.

What makes catechesis exciting at this time in history? Let me be honest. It has little to do with smooth paths or comfortable circumstances. We live in a time of major transitions—demographic, cultural, social, and even political—that demand significant adjustments to how Catholics share our faith.

Recent migration patterns, mainly from Latin America, the Caribbean, Asia, and Africa, among other places, are deeply transforming thousands of faith communities throughout the country. Catholicism in several regions and major cities has become a de facto bilingual (English/Spanish) and bicultural reality, thanks to the incredible growth of the Hispanic population. The rise of social media as a way of life, coupled with the pervasive use of technology, has not only expanded our global awareness but also compelled us to bring the message of Christianity to the virtual worlds that millions of Catholics inhabit.

Many speak of a paradigm change. Yes, a new cultural paradigm has emerged, characterized by diversity. This means that we live in a different context where cultural diversity is the standard for how millions of Catholics in the United States live and practice our faith. Such a shift requires fresher ways of doing catechesis and evangelization that respond to the demands of our culturally diverse contexts. This is a time of challenges and opportunities.

This short book addresses the question of what it means to do catechesis in a culturally diverse church. This question is without a doubt on the minds of many catechists and pastoral leaders in thousands of Catholic parishes, schools, organizations, and groups in every corner of our country. The feelings associated with the topic of cultural diversity often include anxiety, hesitation, puzzlement, skepticism, anger, expectation, and curiosity. It is fine to go through all these emotions since they indicate that we care about how we do catechesis. In fact, they invite some form of engagement. I worry more when there are no feelings at all or no conversations about cultural diversity.

If you are looking here for "solutions" to cultural diversity, then you will be disappointed. This book does not treat cultural diversity as a problem but as an opportunity. Cultural diversity is a unique opportunity to share the Good News of Jesus Christ in new and creative ways while taking the many cultural realities that shape the lives of U.S. Catholics seriously. We are not the first Catholics to do this; most probably, we will not be the last.

In some cases, catechizing in a culturally diverse context requires exploring a new language or learning about a different cultural tradition to better share our faith. Such contexts often require that we empower people from the cultural, linguistic, and racial/ethnic groups that are already present in our faith communities. Because cultural diversity affects us all one way or another, catechists and catechetical leaders in diverse contexts need to develop the appropriate intercultural competencies.

Cultural diversity opens up a new world of possibilities for catechesis and for catechists. It compels us to go beyond the usual ways of doing things. It requires that we use the best of our imagination and wisdom. It takes us out of our comfort zones into spaces that demand new relationships and new pedagogical approaches. This is what makes it exciting!

In the following pages, you will find a combination of reflections and suggestions to catechize and organize catechetical programs in culturally diverse contexts. I draw from several sources. First, my own catechetical experience serving in a trilingual parish for several years, then working at the diocesan level, and currently as a professor of religious education at a Catholic university. Second, from various bodies of literature that inform the arguments presented. Third, and perhaps most important, from the wisdom of countless catechetical and other pastoral leaders from different cultural backgrounds whom I have engaged in dialogue during my travels throughout the country giving presentations and learning from their invaluable experience.

At the end of each chapter there are a few questions for reflection and discussion. I invite you to read or study the book with other people in your group or larger faith community. This topic definitely calls for a good interchange with others.

Hosffman Ospino
JANUARY 31, 2017
FEAST OF SAINT JOHN BOSCO

PART I

Why

Yes, Friends, Cultural Diversity Is Real

Chances are that if you are a Catholic in the United States, you have heard people talking about "cultural diversity." If not, well, you just did! Maybe you are reading this book precisely because someone informed you that catechesis in your faith community from now on needed to be more mindful about cultural diversity.

The expression has become rather popular in conferences, church documents, and programs. Even the Catholic bishops of the United States a few years ago (in 2008) established a large office called the Secretariat of Cultural Diversity in the Church.

But what is it? What do we mean when we talk about cultural diversity? Some catechists and ministerial leaders feel bewildered by these two words. Others are curious. And let's be honest, some are suspicious, perhaps dismissive, because in some corners of our society the terms "culture" and "diversity" are, as they say, loaded politically and ideologically.

To put many hearts and minds at peace, we will not delve into politics or ideology. And to make sure that that remains the case, we must state at the outset that cultural diversity *is not* treated in this book as a "philosophy" (a set of particular ideas that lead us to a set of defined commitments) or an "ideal to be achieved" (i.e., let's make Catholicism in the United States culturally diverse).

In this book, we speak of cultural diversity as *a reality* that already is shaping how the majority of U.S. Catholics live and experience God in the everyday. Yes, the majority! To be Catholic in the United States is to be part of a beautiful experience in which many baptized women and men from different cultures, races, and traditions are all together in parishes, schools, and other faith communities to experience the fullness of the love of Christ and to build the church in the twenty-first century.

A few numbers can help us put things in perspective:

There are about 17,200 parishes in the United States. In nearly 40% of these communities (approx. 7,000), Mass and other services are celebrated in a language other than English, or more than half of parishioners do not self-identify as Euro-American, White. Thousands exhibit both characteristics.

- About 4,500 Catholic parishes in the country explicitly serve Hispanic Catholics, primarily offering services in Spanish.

- The two fastest growing groups of Catholics in the country are Hispanics and Asians.

- More than 50% of Catholics older than 35 are Euro-American, White.

- Six out of ten U.S. Catholics under the age of 18 are Hispanic.

We do not need to imagine cultural diversity or figure out how to be more culturally diverse! Accepting who we are is a good beginning to better understanding our present reality and anticipating where we are heading in the near future. Also, being mindful of these realities will allow us to imagine the kind of catechesis and evangelization needed at this time.

Cultural diversity is a reality that has a direct impact on how we define ourselves as individuals and as members of a community, how we live our faith, and how we pass on the faith to the next generation. "We" in this case is everyone, from all cultures, races, and ethnicities, who self-identifies as Catholic in this country: White, Black, Hispanic, Asian, Pacific Islander, Native American, etc.

As we imagine fresher and creative ways of doing catechesis in a culturally diverse context like Catholicism in the United States of America, we need to have honest conversations that invite us to reflect about

- the importance of the many languages Catholics speak in our own parishes,

- the cultural traditions that help them carry their values and convictions, and

- the ways in which they prefer to share their experience of God.

We are to do this while building *one* church in communion with God and with one another. Tall order, undoubtedly, yet a worthy project! If it is of any consolation, we are not the first Catholics in the history of the United States to have that responsibility.

EARLIER WAVES OF CATHOLIC MIGRATION

Catholicism in the United States from its very beginning has been sustained by the faithfulness, creativity, and the tenacity of immigrants from various parts of the world.

The first Catholics in what is now U.S. territory came from Spain, more than two centuries before the nation was founded. They settled mainly in the South and the West, and some in the Southeast as well as in the Caribbean. There they established missions that served as religious and educational centers for the local communities. As time went by, most of these missions closed and ceased having much influence upon how Catholics were evangelized.

French Catholics grew roots and built churches in the old Louisiana Territory. Some grew roots in the Northern part of the country close to other French immigrants who settled in what today we know as Canada. As territories with a large presence of French Catholics formally became part of the United States, elements of the French culture became part of the social fabric of their communities.

Black Catholics constituted a small, yet significant presence in the church between the sixteenth and nineteenth centuries. Unfortunately the negative effects of slavery and racial discrimination prevented this population from fully integrating into the church and flourishing. Many of those effects are still felt in our day.

During the nineteenth century, in the years after the U.S. became an independent nation, millions of Catholics, mainly from Western Europe, arrived on U.S. shores and settled primarily in the Northeast and Midwest. Many others went to other parts of the young, expanding nation. Millions more would arrive in later decades. By the middle of the twentieth century, more than 23,000 parishes, more than 13,000 Catholic schools, and thousands of other structures, including hospitals and universities, served as evidence of a strong Catholic presence and contributions to the larger U.S. society. Catholics became the largest church in the country. Today, a full quarter of all people in the United States self-identifies as Catholic.

Worth highlighting is the role of *national parishes* as these immigrants settled. The majority of European Catholic immigrants during this century and a half did not arrive speaking English. As they built parishes to worship and sustain their faith, they were able to use their native languages. Italian Catholics established Italian parishes, German Catholics German parishes, Polish Catholics Polish parishes, and so on. While formal liturgies were in Latin (before the liturgical renewal brought about by the Second Vatican Council), homilies, catechesis, missions, evangelization programs, and outreach initiatives were usually offered in the language of the immigrants.

This was an example of cultural diversity at its best. National parishes, and what happened in them, provided creative responses to cultural diversity instead of resisting it. National parishes were true cultural and linguistic oases for these immigrants and their families. These parishes played a major role in supporting the relationship between faith and culture.

As the immigration waves from Europe dwindled and the children and grandchildren of immigrants became more integrated into U.S. culture, the use of languages other than English became less common. National parishes also stopped defining their role as places serving primarily immigrants. Most became regular territorial parishes offering services and catechesis in English to a mostly U.S.-born Catholic population. Many closed.

NEW MIGRATION PATTERNS IN THE CONTEXT OF GLOBALIZATION
If there is something that we know for certain, it is that history never stops—well, technically it will at the end of times! But for now, we are part of this continuum.

Between the early 1800s until the middle of the twentieth century, U.S. Catholicism was profoundly shaped by the efforts and experiences of European Catholic immigrants and their descendants. Much of that experience became constitutive to what many understand as mainstream U.S. Catholicism in our day.

The second part of the twentieth century brought many changes to the United States of America as a nation and to thousands of Catholic communities throughout the territory. Just naming the impact of major movements and revolutions during the 1960s, for instance, would take a long book—or perhaps an entire collection of books! And this is just one decade.

To better appreciate the context in which U.S. Catholics live today, we need to look at two sets of realities that have profoundly impacted our country—and much of the world—during the last half a century: *globalization* and *new migration patterns*. Both have had serious impact upon U.S. Catholicism and how we define cultural diversity.

1. Globalization and its Effects. Have you ever had the feeling that the world is changing too fast and that you are having a hard time keeping up with it? Well, you are not imagining it. It is changing fast, and it is practically impossible to keep up with all the changes!

Contemporary developments in technology and increasingly faster means of transportation have made our world feel smaller. These have deeply transformed how we relate to our immediate reality and to others. The use of the internet has placed the world at our fingertips. Thanks to the World Wide Web we live permanently "connected." Social media spaces (e.g., Facebook) are the new public squares where people live, share their thoughts, and search for meaning. Cell phones have enhanced uniquely the way in which we communicate: each person has his or her own number and can be reached virtually everywhere. Smart phones and tablets allow us to carry small, yet powerful computing machines that provide countless services and have led us to think that we cannot live without them. All these developments have in turn deeply reshaped how we receive, process, create, save, and discard information.

One does not have to be too old to notice how much these realities have redefined behavior. If you are in your thirties or older, most likely you lived in a time when no smart phones, internet, or Facebook were available to the public. How can one live without them today!

It is not news that we live in a world with interdependent economies. One sneeze in the Asian markets or Wall Street can send the entire global financial system spinning in many directions. Something similar applies to the political world. An internal conflict, a natural disaster, or the rise of a particular political leader in a distant nation can trigger chain reactions that may lead millions to migrate or entire social structures to crumble in rather short periods of time.

What is the impact of these realities upon the way we do catechesis? Three shifts are worthy of consideration:

SHIFT I. Influenced by contemporary cultural realities, U.S. Catholics, especially the young, are more comfortable than ever receiving, processing, creating, saving, and discarding religious information. Catechesis cannot limit itself to merely communicating rote content from a catechism or a book, or listening to someone in a position of authority. It needs to be a process that truly engages people's lives here and now, their ability to process information that is readily accessible (e.g., if someone has a question about religion, it is most likely that they would go to Google than to a priest or a catechist!), their questions, and the tools that they use to interpret the world.

SHIFT 2. People's lives today are deeply shaped by the use of technology, the internet, and social media. We would fool ourselves if we think that catechesis should only happen at church on weekends or in a school setting. If we want to "connect" with contemporary Catholics as catechists, we must learn how to use these resources to share the Good News. We must join and be present in the spaces that they inhabit.

SHIFT 3. People in our day possess a heightened sensibility about global dynamics. For some, this is the result of constantly being exposed to news, friends, and even relatives whose lives are directly impacted by global economic or political realities. For others, it is about their own lives. About seventeen million Catholics in the United States are immigrants, exiles, or refugees. A catechesis that fails to make global connections in our day runs the risk of becoming irrelevant. Catechesis cannot ignore the reasons for which immigrants left their home countries, the cultures and languages in which they learned their faith, and the ways in which they build community in parishes, neighborhoods, and homes as they start a new life in the U.S.

Perhaps this is not how you first thought that a book on catechesis and cultural diversity in the United States would start. Yet globalization dynamics have much to do with the cultural transformations of our time. The realities just described are forging new ways of being American and Catholic that catechists and catechetical leaders need to keep in mind as we plan our ministries.

2. New Migration Patterns. The most recent waves of Catholic immigrants who have arrived in the United States have done so in the context of the globalization dynamics just described. This time, most immigrants do not come from Europe but from Latin America, Asia, and Africa.

The largest number of Catholic immigrants that has arrived in the country comes from Latin America and the Caribbean. Because of their historical, cultural, and linguistic background, they are grouped under the category Hispanic or Latino. The impact of this group upon the U.S. Catholic experience is not small: Hispanics account for 71% of the growth of U.S. Catholicism since 1960!

Hispanic immigrants and their children join millions of Hispanics who became part of the United States at various points in history and for various reasons. In 1848, half of the Mexican territory became part of the United States — much of the Southwest. Most Hispanics are Mexican American and Mexican. In 1898 Puerto Rico was annexed as a colony, making Puerto Ricans the second largest group of Hispanics in the country.

Millions of Catholics from Latin America and the Caribbean have arrived in the United States as part of a decades-long immigration wave. It is estimated that about one million new Latin American immigrants make the U.S. their home every year, most of them Catholic. The reasons for this continuous migration vary. The geographical proximity to the U.S. certainly plays a major role. Millions arrive searching for better opportunities for themselves and their families; others are fleeing war and violence; some have to leave because of political instability; others lost everything in natural disasters. Many arrive as part of family reunification policies. The reasons are very similar to those that prompted millions of European Catholics to seek the United States as a new home not long ago.

During the second part of the twentieth century, hundreds of thousands of Catholic immigrants from Asia and Africa also arrived in the United States. Though the impact of their presence is smaller compared to that of Hispanics, thousands of communities are being transformed by their presence, cultural traditions, and the many ways in which they practice Catholicism.

It is important to take into consideration the fact that although large percentages of Hispanic, Asian, and African Catholic adults in the United States are immigrants, the majority of their children are U.S.-born. These children and young people, nonetheless, are being raised in immigrant households, being introduced to the faith and their relationship with Jesus Christ by their immigrant parents and relatives. Catechesis and evangelization efforts should not ignore the immigrant influence upon how millions of Catholics in the country live and practice their faith.

As immigrants and their children grow roots in U.S. culture, they are also appropriating what we can call "the American way" of doing things. That includes learning the common language, embracing practices, and using the tools that shape the lives of people in this country every day.

Learning a culture and making it one's own is part of the natural process of integration that every group undergoes. Such a process of integration requires some negotiation of cultural identities. In the past, immigrants were often encouraged to leave behind their old cultural selves to become fully Americanized. Most likely this never happened fully since that would be the equivalent to self-denial at the most intimate level. Yet, some tried by limiting the use of languages other than English to the home or other private contexts, including church. Some embraced practices and attitudes perceived to be more American to fit into the larger society. Today, Americanization is not necessarily defined in terms of abandoning particular cultural roots and traditions—even though some sectors of society still wrestle with how to deal with difference. In fact, one of the traits of American culture is precisely the open embrace of cultural diversity as a way of life. It is okay to be American, Catholic, and... White, Hispanic, Black, Asian, etc.

A picture of Catholicism in the United States in terms of racial/ethnic backgrounds today would look like this (the percentages are approximations):

EURO-AMERICAN, WHITE	47%
HISPANIC	43%
ASIAN / PACIFIC ISLANDER	5%
AFRICAN AMERICAN/BLACK	4%
NATIVE AMERICAN	1%

This is a significantly different picture compared to U.S. Catholicism in the 1950s when Euro-American, White Catholics constituted about 90% of all Catholics in the country and Hispanics barely reached 6%!

U.S. Catholicism in the twenty-first century will be profoundly defined by how we catechize and support this culturally diverse body of Catholics and accompany them in building strong communities of faith.

THE MULTICULTURAL PARISH

As indicated earlier, national parishes played a major role in helping European Catholic immigrants settle and grow in their faith in the new country. When these immigrants arrived, there were no parishes in most parts of the country. They built them and used them as spaces to nurture their faith and their particular cultures.

The new wave of Catholic immigrants from Latin America, Asia, and Africa are settling in the midst of much different circumstances. On the one hand, upon their arrival they encounter more than 17,000 Catholic parishes that are relatively well established and organized. The most natural move for these immigrants is to worship in these places. After all, a healthy ecclesiology suggests that parishes are built to serve the People of God, not just one specific group.

Let's keep in mind, also, that most growth for Catholicism in the United States is taking place not in the Northeast and the Midwest, where the previous wave of immigrant Catholics settled a century or so ago. Most Hispanic and Asian Catholics live in the South and the West, where there are fewer parishes and schools. New Catholic parishes, schools, and other structures will likely need to be built in the near future as Catholicism continues to grow roots in these regions.

In the United States, most Catholics receive pastoral care in territorial parishes. It is the responsibility of every local parish to serve the pastoral and spiritual needs of all Catholics in its territory. This implies adjusting to cultural and linguistic needs of Catholics when needed.

These details provide Catholics with important information to speak of the nuances of cultural diversity in our day. As indicated earlier, we are not talking about a philosophy or an ideal goal to be accomplished. Cultural diversity is about who we are as a church in the twenty-first century. It is the experience of entering into relationship with God as Catholics in a context where people from many cultures, who speak many languages and have many ways of practicing their Catholic faith, come together in parishes and other faith communities to build the church.

So cultural diversity is not an option. This may sound harsh and perhaps uncomfortable. But we cannot "opt out" of cultural diversity. We cannot opt out of who we are unless we want to segregate our communities or run the risk of becoming irrelevant to the next generation of U.S. Catholics. To be Catholic in the United States is to participate in an experience that compels us to admit that culture, language, race/ethnicity, and social location matter. To be Catholic in the United States is to acknowledge that people make sense of their faith in ways that are shaped by multiple cultural perspectives.

Now we must ask how cultural diversity calls for fresher and creative ways of doing catechesis. The following chapters will engage this question in various ways. But for now, we need to make three affirmations:

First, we need catechetical initiatives and resources that intentionally honor the multiple cultural expressions and traditions in which Catholics in the United States practice their faith. This includes recognizing the influence of global dynamics as we negotiate our identities as Americans and Catholics.

Second, we need catechists who are respectful of the diversity of cultural perspectives that give life to Catholics in our country, humbly acknowledging that each of us traces our roots to particular cultural traditions.

Third, we need a catechesis that helps the baptized to build communities of faith deeply rooted in gospel values and the best of our tradition while authentically embracing all Catholics regardless of their origin, immigration status, skin color, language, or cultural background.

● *Questions for Dialogue and Reflection*

- In your own words, what is cultural diversity?

- What caught your attention about how Catholic immigrants have settled in the United States at various points in history?

- What would you say are some of the main characteristics of American Catholicism?

- What obstacles do you see to Catholics embracing cultural diversity?

A Few Thoughts
on Culture

As we speak about cultural diversity, it seems appropriate to take a moment and explain the term "culture." In principle, it seems like an easy task. All one needs to do is offer a definition that captures the meaning of the word in a way that most people can understand and be satisfied with.

The challenge is that arriving at such a definition is actually not that easy. Many people, including Catholic scholars, philosophers, theologians, educators, and even catechists, have attempted to define culture in various ways. The library of the university where I teach has entire bookshelves filled with books about culture. I have found books dedicated to collecting and comparing definitions of culture from different perspectives.

Do not worry. I am not going to walk you through all these definitions or delve into the details of those conversations. All we need to know at this point is that when we speak about culture, we are speaking about something complex.

Some approaches to culture have been significantly influential throughout time. For instance, one can understand culture as belonging to a certain social lineage (e.g., nobility), having a privileged social position, or even having citizenship. In this case, to have culture means to belong to a particular sector of society with some form of political, financial, and even religious influence. The biggest limitation of this understanding is that it lends itself to elitism.

Sometimes culture is understood as educational or professional attainment, or perhaps expertise and recognition in a particular area of life (e.g., art, politics, academic activity). The persons or groups who achieve such expertise are perceived as "cultured," while everyone else is not. Once again, elitism lurks, since this definition tends to acknowledge only some forms of expertise. It also ignores social circumstances that prevent certain groups from being educated and from sharing their gifts with the larger whole.

Quite often, the term "culture" points to artifacts such as artistic and literary works, among many other expressions of human ingenuity. These external productions reflect ideas and convictions, traditions and worldviews. Nonetheless, this definition can limit the idea of culture mainly to what we can perceive with our senses.

This is just a sample of possibilities. My hope is that you understand the magnitude of the task!

It always helps to keep in mind that there are visible and invisible elements of culture. Sometimes we limit our understanding of culture to what we perceive most immediately: food, music, language, etc. It is easy to construct cultural stereotypes based just on what we "see." However, there is much more to culture that we do not see: values, stories, convictions, principles, biases, hopes, and more.

Scholars of culture often use the image of an iceberg to illustrate the reality of culture. Say the iceberg represents a particular culture. The top of the iceberg, what we see, is important but not the entire whole. In fact, the largest part of the iceberg is under water, invisible, yet it is what sustains what we see. Something similar happens with culture. We need to take the time to learn about and appreciate what we do not see.

We need a more comprehensive definition of culture.

A CATHOLIC APPROACH TO CULTURE

As long as there are people naming and interpreting what it means to be human, most likely the number of definitions of culture will continue to expand.

Catholics have been very active in this conversation. After all, we need to have a basic understanding of culture to explain who we are and how we relate to God in the context of history. We need a foundational definition of culture to determine how sharing faith makes a difference in our communities and particular groups. Besides, a good understanding of culture is important to inspire our imagination to bring life to faith and faith to life.

The Second Vatican Council (1962-1965), undoubtedly the best roadmap for Catholics to advance catechesis and evangelization in our day, has been instrumental in this regard. The Council provided an important framework for Catholics to interpret the relationship between faith and culture:

> The joys and the hopes, the griefs and the anxieties of
> the men of this age, especially those who are poor or
> in any way afflicted, these are the joys and hopes, the
> griefs and anxieties of the followers of Christ.
> PASTORAL CONSTITUTION ON THE CHURCH IN THE MODERN
> WORLD, *Gaudium et Spes*, N. I

In light of this conviction, Vatican II proposed an integral understanding of culture that affirms the spiritual and material, intellectual and emotional, individual and social dimensions of our human existence:

> The word "culture" in its general sense indicates everything whereby man develops and perfects his many bodily and spiritual qualities; he strives by his knowledge and his labor, to bring the world itself under his control. He renders social life more human both in the family and the civic community, through improvement of customs and institutions. Throughout the course of time he expresses, communicates and conserves in his works, great spiritual experiences and desires, that they might be of advantage to the progress of many, even of the whole human family. ***Gaudium et Spes*, N. 53**

This definition does not necessarily say it all, because our theology is very rich and we could add many more elements, but it offers a comprehensive understanding of the term. Perhaps the biggest strength of this definition of culture is that the starting point is the human person in relationship with God, others, and the world.

That means that when we speak about culture as Catholics, we must consider at least three core elements:

1. Our vocation—into existence and to salvation—is from God;

2. We live that vocation as children of God in our particular cultural contexts; and

3. Our purpose is to achieve fulfillment in what we do within culture, working for a better world for all—while longing for the hope of eternity, promised and anticipated in Jesus Christ.

A FEW ESSENTIALS ABOUT CULTURE

The integral definition of culture provided by *Gaudium et Spes* allows us to make some fundamental assertions:

First, culture is an essential element of the human experience. God comes to our encounter in history in the context of culture.

Second, every human being belongs to a particular cultural reality. There is no one who is "culture-less." We all belong somewhere.

Third, culture is like a matrix within which we make meaning about who we are, learn the basic tools to interpret the world, and engage in relationships with others, God, and the world (e.g., language, symbols, rituals).

Fourth, large cultural realities often contain subcultures that allow individuals and groups to live their human experience and religious convictions in the comfort of some particularity. For instance, we can speak of the American Catholic culture as a large reality that holds particular cultural expressions such as Hispanic Catholicism, African-American Catholicism, Euro-American Catholicism, Asian-American-Catholicism, and Native-American Catholicism. These particular expressions may highlight certain elements of the larger culture and not others. They may simultaneously live in tension while complementing one another. They cross boundaries, challenge each other, and enrich the larger whole. Each could even have particular expressions within their own worlds (e.g., Puerto Rican Catholics and Mexican-American Catholics bring to life the Hispanic Catholic experience in unique ways).

Fifth, although we all belong to particular cultural communities where our worldviews are constantly shaped, we can transition in between cultural worlds, learn new ones, and leave old ones behind. In our fast-moving world, people regularly transition from one cultural world to another, constantly negotiating identities.

IMPLICATIONS FOR CATECHESIS

Let us take these five essential convictions and place them in the context of catechesis in culturally diverse contexts, as is the case in thousands of parishes, schools, and other Catholic communities throughout the United States.

Catechists who take culture seriously must acknowledge that...

a. Culture matters. We should not underestimate the importance of cultural location.

b. Catechesis cannot take place outside the specific cultural worlds and realities that shape the lives of Catholics. Even when we speak and teach, we do it out of a specific cultural perspective.

c. The only way to share our faith with others is by using the basic cultural tools with which they interpret the world and engage in relationships (e.g., language, symbols, rituals). No effective communication is possible without those basic cultural tools.

d. Cultures are neither homogeneous nor static. Cultures are complex and in flux. It is fine that several cultural perspectives coexist in a relationship of tension and mutual complementarity.

e. People are constantly negotiating identities as they transition from one cultural context to another, even as they discern and practice their faith. Catechesis is a perfect opportunity to discuss those transitions to help them understand how God walks with them on their journey.

❂ *Questions for Dialogue and Reflection*

- If someone asked you, "What is your culture?", how would you describe it?

- What are some negative understandings about culture that prevail in our society or in your faith community? (Name one or two). How would you respond in light of what you read in this chapter?

- Name the particular way of living Catholicism in the United States in light of the cultural background that identifies you best. Using the image of the iceberg, name some of the visible elements and some of the invisible ones that identify your cultural way of living American Catholicism. What did you learn from this exercise?

- What possibilities for catechesis and evangelization open up when we acknowledge that, although we all believe in the same Jesus Christ and belong to the same church, there are different cultural ways of living Catholicism in the United States?

From Our Own Catholic Wells

The commitment to embracing culture as an important aspect of catechesis and evangelization dates back to the early days of Christianity. As Catholics, we hold the conviction that the gospel can enter into the heart of a culture and transform it from within with the power of the Holy Spirit. The conviction evokes the mystery of God's Word who becomes flesh in the person of Jesus of Nazareth, assuming the fullness of humanity to redeem and save us.

The encounter between the gospel and culture(s) has profound implications for the salvation of humanity. God saves us in Jesus Christ in the context of the cultural realities that shape our lives.

Some catechists may get the impression that Catholics in the United States are overly engaged in the conversation about how faith and culture relate as we share our faith. Perhaps we do this because of the high levels of cultural diversity that currently shape the lives of our communities. It is possible that some also think that the interest in cultural diversity comes from a sector of the church that is concerned with social and political dynamics that have little or nothing to do with announcing the gospel and sharing the richness of the Christian tradition.

Neither observation is fully accurate. On the one hand, cultural diversity is hardly a U.S. phenomenon. It is the experience of hundreds of millions of Catholics throughout the world who contend with different expressions of cultural pluralism on a daily basis. Just imagine being a Christian and organizing a catechetical program in Asia where barely seven percent of the entire population self-identifies as such!

On the other hand, the reflection about how culture shapes catechesis and evangelization has deep spiritual and theological roots. At the heart of the catechetical experience, Catholics constantly explore how faith forms, informs, and transforms our lives through the encounter with Jesus Christ. Catechesis does not happen in a vacuum. When Catholics engage in the catechetical experience, we bring all we are, including our faith, our culture, our politics, and our relationships.

To help catechists reading this book get a sense of how Catholics reflect about the relationship between catechesis and culture, I have selected the following quotes from a variety of church documents written at different points during the last half century. One of my colleagues, Dr. Jane Regan, regularly affirms that "documents are our friends." I think that she is right.

Most of the following quotes come from documents written for the entire church, with the exception of those taken from the United States *National Directory for Catechesis*. These quotes are a great resource to support arguments about the importance of fostering catechetical experiences that take cultural diversity seriously.

CULTURE MATTERS

The following excerpts underscore the Catholic Church's recognition of the value of culture and the part it plays in our efforts to evangelize and catechize.

> When properly understood, cultural diversity
> is not a threat to Church unity.
> POPE FRANCIS, *Evangelii Gaudium* (2013), N. 117

> What matters is to evangelize [people's] culture and
> cultures (not in a purely decorative way, as it were, by
> applying a thin veneer, but in a vital way, in depth and
> right to their very roots)...always taking the person
> as one's starting-point and always coming back to the
> relationships of people among themselves and with
> God. POPE PAUL VI, *Evangelii Nuntiandi* (1975), N. 20

> Every dimension of the faith, like the faith itself as
> a whole, must be rooted in human experience and
> not remain a mere adjunct to the human person.
> Knowledge of the faith is significant. It gives light
> to the whole of existence and dialogues with culture.
> *General Directory for Catechesis* (1997), N. 87

CULTURE, CATECHESIS AND EVANGELIZATION GO HAND IN HAND

Our catechetical documents place catechesis within the broader context of evangelization. One of the most effective ways to solidify this connection is through attention to the diversity of culture within the church.

> We can say of catechesis, as well as of evangelization
> in general, that it is called to bring the power of the
> Gospel into the very heart of culture and cultures.

For this purpose, catechesis will seek to know these cultures and their essential components; it will learn their most significant expressions; it will respect their particular values and riches.

POPE JOHN PAUL II, *Catechesi Tradendae* (1979), N. 53

All the baptized, because they are called by God to maturity of faith, need and have therefore a right to adequate catechesis. It is thus a primary responsibility of the Church to respond to this in a fitting and satisfactory manner. Hence it must be recalled that those to be evangelized are "concrete and historical persons," rooted in a given situation and always influenced by pedagogical, social, cultural, and religious conditioning. *General Directory for Catechesis* (1997), N. 167

The profession of faith received by the Church (*traditio*), which germinates and grows during the catechetical process, is given back (*redditio*), enriched by the values of different cultures.
General Directory for Catechesis (1997), N. 78

Local catechisms, prepared or approved by diocesan Bishops or by Episcopal Conferences, are invaluable instruments for catechesis which are "called to bring the power of the Gospel into the very heart of culture and cultures." *General Directory for Catechesis* (1997), N. 131

CATECHESIS AND INCULTURATION

There is no "one-size-fits-all" approach to catechesis, particularly when it comes to the recognition of the role of cultural diversity in the process. Adaptation is essential in order to catechize in a culturally diverse church.

The People of God is incarnate in the peoples of the earth, each of which has its own culture...The human person is always situated in a culture: "nature and culture are intimately linked." Grace supposes culture, and God's gift becomes flesh in the culture of those who receive it.

POPE FRANCIS, *Evangelii Gaudium* (2013), N. 115

Once the Gospel has been inculturated in a people, in their process of transmitting their culture they also transmit the faith in ever new forms; hence the importance of understanding evangelization as inculturation.

POPE FRANCIS, *Evangelii Gaudium* (2013), N. 122

The "adaptation of the preaching of the revealed word must always remain a law for all evangelization." There is an intrinsic theological motivation for this in the Incarnation. [The Church] sets out to meet each person, taking into serious account diversity of circumstances and cultures and maintains the unity of so many in the one saving Word.

General Directory for Catechesis (1997), N. 169

Adaptation is realized in accordance with the diverse circumstances in which the word of God is transmitted. These are determined by "differences of culture, age, spiritual maturity and social and ecclesial conditions amongst all of those to whom it is addressed." Much careful attention shall be given to them. *General Directory for Catechesis* (1997), N. 170

In the diversity of peoples who experience the gift of God, each in accordance with its own culture, the

Church expresses her genuine catholicity and shows forth the "beauty of her varied face." In the Christian customs of an evangelized people, the Holy Spirit adorns the Church, showing her new aspects of revelation and giving her a new face. Through inculturation, the Church "introduces peoples, together with their cultures, into her own community," for "every culture offers positive values and forms which can enrich the way the Gospel is preached, understood and lived."

POPE FRANCIS, *Evangelii Gaudium* (2013), N. 116

CATECHESIS AND CULTURAL DIVERSITY IN THE UNITED STATES

The *National Directory for Catechesis* draws upon the overall catechetical vision of the church and makes specific application to the Catholic Church in the United States. The following excerpts thus underscore the reality of cultural pluralism as an integral part of the American experience.

Since persons can only achieve their full humanity by means of culture, the Catholic Church in the United States embraces the rich cultural pluralism of all the faithful, encourages the distinctive identity of each cultural group, and urges mutual enrichment. At the same time, the Catholic Church promotes a unity of faith within the multicultural diversity of the people.

USCCB, *National Directory for Catechesis* (2005), CHAPTER I, II.C.I

The diversity of ethnicity, education, and social status challenges the Church to integrate the new immigrants in ways that both respect their diverse cultures and experiences of Church and enrich both the immigrants and the Church. The Church of the twenty-first century in the United States will be a Church of many cultures, languages, and traditions—yet one in faith.

USCCB, *National Directory for Catechesis* (2005),
CHAPTER I, II.C.I

If catechesis is to be effective, all those responsible for it must monitor the rapid changes in social and cultural trends. The catechist must be able to introduce the real person of Jesus Christ to the real persons of this time and place in history.

USCCB, *National Directory for Catechesis* (2005), CHAPTER I, 14

DUTIES OF CATECHESIS FOR INCULTURATION OF THE FAITH

These duties form an organic whole and are briefly expressed as follows:

• to know in depth the culture of persons and the extent of its penetration into their lives;

• to recognize a cultural dimension in the Gospel itself, while affirming, on the one hand, that this does not spring from some human cultural *humus,* and recognizing, on the other, that the Gospel cannot be isolated from the cultures in which it was initially inserted and in which it has found expression through the centuries;

• to proclaim the profound change, the conversion, which the Gospel, as a "transforming and regenerating" force works in culture;

• to witness to the transcendence and the non-exhaustion of the Gospel with regard to culture, while at the same time discerning those seeds of the Gospel which may be present in culture;

• to promote a new expression of the Gospel in accordance with evangelized culture, looking to a language of the faith which is the common patrimony of the faithful and thus a fundamental element of communion;

• to maintain integrally the content of the faith and ensure that the doctrinal formulations of tradition are explained and illustrated, while taking into account the cultural and historical circumstances of those being instructed, and to avoid defacing or falsifying the contents.

General Directory for Catechesis (2017), N. 203

CATECHETICAL CARE OF IMMIGRANTS

The Catholic Church has long advocated for the welfare of immigrants. Coming as they do from various cultures, immigrants require the kind of pastoral care and catechetical outreach that both values their heritage and supports their efforts to assimilate into a larger culture.

Pastoral care of migrants means welcome, respect, protection, promotion and genuine love of every person in his or her religious and cultural expressions.

PONTIFICAL COUNCIL FOR THE PASTORAL CARE OF MIGRANTS AND ITINERANT PEOPLE, INSTRUCTION, *The Love of Christ towards Migrants*, N. 28

Those responsible for pastoral work among migrants should thus have a certain expertise in intercultural communication.

PONTIFICAL COUNCIL FOR THE PASTORAL CARE OF MIGRANTS AND ITINERANT PEOPLE, INSTRUCTION, *The Love of Christ towards Migrants*, **N. 78**

Being communion, the Church values the legitimate specific characteristics of Catholic communities, joining them together with a universal vision. In fact the unity of Pentecost does not abolish the various languages and cultures but recognizes them in their identities, at the same time opening them to other realities through the universal love at work in them.

PONTIFICAL COUNCIL FOR THE PASTORAL CARE OF MIGRANTS AND ITINERANT PEOPLE, INSTRUCTION, *The Love of Christ towards Migrants*, **N. 37.1**

The uprooting that moving abroad inevitably involves (from country of origin, family, language, etc.) should not be made worse by uprooting the migrant from his religious rite or identity too.

PONTIFICAL COUNCIL FOR THE PASTORAL CARE OF MIGRANTS AND ITINERANT PEOPLE, INSTRUCTION, *The Love of Christ towards Migrants*, **N. 49**

[The catechesis of the marginalized] addresses itself to immigrants, refugees, nomads, travelling people... Permanent signs of the strength of catechesis are its capacity to identify different situations, to meet the needs and questions of everyone, to stress the value of generous and patient personal contact, to proceed with trust and realism, sometimes turning to indirect and occasional forms of catechesis.

General Directory for Catechesis (1997), N. 190

CATECHESIS AND LANGUAGE DIVERSITY

Many parishes are making an effort to incorporate the native languages of their culturally diverse communities in liturgical celebrations. Similar efforts need to be made for our catechetical efforts as well.

Catechesis is a basic evangelizing activity of every particular Church. By means of it the Diocese gives to all its members, and to all who come with a desire to give themselves to Jesus Christ, a formative process which permits knowledge, celebration, living and proclamation within a particular cultural horizon. In this way the confession of faith—the goal of catechesis—can be proclaimed by the disciples of Christ "in their own tongues." As at Pentecost, so also today, the Church of Christ, "present and operative" (138) in the particular Churches, "speaks all languages," since like a growing tree she extends her roots into all cultures.

General Directory for Catechesis (2017), N. 218

CATECHESIS IS TO RAISE AWARENESS
ABOUT SOCIO-CULTURAL REALITIES

Catechists have the potential to embody the call to justice and to instill in those they catechize a commitment to inclusion and peace.

In the context of catechesis above all it is important that the teaching of the Church's social doctrine be directed towards motivating action for the evangelization and humanization of temporal realities. Through this doctrine, in fact, the Church expresses a theoretical and practical knowledge that gives support to the commitment of transforming social life, helping it to conform ever more fully to the divine plan. Social catechesis aims at the formation of men and women who, in their respect for the moral order, are lovers of true freedom, people who "will form their own judgments in the light of truth, direct their activities with a sense of responsibility, and strive for what is true and just in willing cooperation with others."

PONTIFICAL COUNCIL FOR JUSTICE AND PEACE,
Compendium of the Social Doctrine of the Church (2004), N. 530

Questions for Dialogue and Reflection

- What is your immediate impression after reading the quotes from church documents in this chapter addressing the relationship between catechesis and culture?

- Pope Francis asserts: "Cultural diversity is not a threat to Church unity." How would you explain this to a group of Catholics who think that too much emphasis on cultural diversity is an obstacle to unity?

- The Pontifical Council for the Pastoral Care of Migrants and Itinerant People reminds us that the "Pastoral care of migrants means welcome, respect, protection, promotion and genuine love of every person in his or her religious and cultural expressions." How are you doing this for the immigrants of your community (if there are any) or the Catholics who are from a cultural tradition different from yours?

■ What kind of catechesis is necessary to create an authentic culture of mutual care and "genuine love" in our diverse faith communities?

God's Way

How does one know that God became present in history and revealed something of importance to all humanity? Let us turn to the Scriptures.

Israel in the Hebrew Scriptures (or Old Testament) is one among many peoples, with its particular history, cultural traditions, language, values, stories, convictions, rituals, politics, and social norms. What makes Israel unique, and relevant to the study of culture, is that the God of the Judeo-Christian revelation chose to enter in direct relationship with them. In doing so, God engages all these characteristics of Israel, including its cultural particularities, sometimes affirming them, sometimes challenging them.

Jesus, the Word made flesh, became one of us in a particular culture: Judaism about two millennia ago. Jesus was born and lived his entire life as a Jewish man. The first Christians were mainly Jews who had recognized Jesus of Nazareth as the Messiah, the anointed one, the fulfillment of God's promises to Israel. They were the first witnesses of the resurrection and committed to building communities rooted in their faith in the Risen One. The Scriptures that we hold as sacred were written in the context of a profoundly Jewish culture.

It is not surprising then that Christianity, even to this day, retains core characteristics of the Jewish cultural and religious tradition. It is not surprising either that in the early years of the Christian era, many people could not differentiate Christians from Jews at first sight, at least culturally! Both had many cultural elements in common. Religion was most likely the main factor that allowed for clear distinctions, particularly the belief in the risen Christ among Christians, but one would need to understand well the theological positions of each community to appreciate the nuances. As Christianity expanded its geographical horizons and grew roots in many other cultures, the distinctions would become more palpable.

Judaism and Christianity are not religious traditions emerging from private revelations to a few select individuals, who in turn processed and communicated what they received to everyone else. Neither are they philosophies resulting from logical deductions by wisdom figures. Both traditions are the testimony of entire communities engaged in a process of intimate relationship with the One God, the God of revelation, who chooses to be in intimate relationship with them.

If God chose freely and gratuitously to enter in relationship with particular communities that are socially and historically located, such engagement could not have happened outside of culture (or cultures). Consequently, it is important for catechists and evangelizers to acknowledge that God's revelation to humanity—at least in its public expression—comes to us through specific cultural embodiments.

Culture plays a significant role in giving us what is necessary to understand...

- what God wants to communicate to humanity (i.e., message);

- how humanity understands God (i.e., the mystery of God); and

- the ways in which we see ourselves in relationship with God (i.e., the mystery of the human person in history).

WORDS AND DEEDS

The Second Vatican Council in its Constitution on Divine Revelation (also known as *Dei Verbum*) reminds us that it is part of God's divine plan to become present to humanity in history through *words* and *deeds*. The document affirms:

> This plan of revelation is realized by deeds and words having an inner unity: the deeds wrought by God in the history of salvation manifest and confirm the teaching and realities signified by the words, while the words proclaim the deeds and clarify the mystery contained in them. N. 2

How fascinating! God chose to become known to humanity "through words and deeds as the one true and living God" (N. 14). So does the Lord Jesus, who "perfected revelation by fulfilling it through his whole work of making himself present and manifesting himself: through his words and deeds, his signs and wonders, but especially through his death and glorious resurrection from the dead and final sending of the Spirit of truth" (N. 4).

The statement that God's revelation happens through words and deeds is very significant. In the context of our everyday experience, words draw from very specific cultural frameworks that give them meaning and make them effective. Without a community of interpreters shaped by a particular cultural framework, words end up being empty sounds.

To understand the assertion "God is love," we must have listeners who understand the meaning of those words in the English language. If the person who hears them does not speak English, no matter how profound and inspirational is their meaning, they will fall on deaf ears.

Let's not forget, however, that human words and concepts most of the time fall short of capturing the fullness and depth of God's mystery. Words are approximations; windows into that mystery. When using words about God and about our faith, we normally use analogies available to us.

For instance, the expression "reign of God" will be understood differently depending on the culture in which it is used. If one has never been exposed to the government of a king or a queen, most likely the expression will mean something different in comparison to someone who has. Words allow us to affirm something about God and God's revealed message within the limits of our cultural experience.

There are some words and concepts in every language and culture that say a lot about how people experience God. Sometimes those words and concepts do not translate well into other languages. Learning different languages and cultures is an opportunity to expand our own horizons of meaning while discovering newer and exciting ways of being in relationship with God.

God acts in history in many ways: God chooses a people, liberates them, loves them, and promises them a Messiah who will bring salvation, among many other actions. God makes sure that there is a community that in light of its cultural, social, and historical experience understands what it means to be chosen, liberated, loved, and saved.

In light of the experience of the resurrection, Jesus Christ constitutes a community of believers who know themselves as children of God, celebrate the Eucharist, proclaim the Good

News to all the nations, work vigorously to build God's reign here and now, and practice God's merciful love, recognizing the face of Christ in their neighbor, especially those most in need.

God's Holy Spirit leads the disciples of the Lord into many cultures to be leaven of God's reign through these actions, allowing the gospel to grow roots in these cultures, and calling those who live in these cultures to experience the gift of salvation.

A DIVINE PEDAGOGY

What we see here is a perfect example of a catechesis that engages culture and affirms the value of cultural particularity to communicate the divine message. The Great Catechist: God!

God does not ignore the specific cultural realities that shape the lives of women and men throughout history. Revelation is communicated in language—words, symbols, insights, actions—that we understand, communally and individually. God as Catechist makes sure that humanity can understand what is being communicated. The message must be understood so it does not get lost.

God's pedagogical approach is profoundly personal and intimate. God reveals the divine plan for humanity, the desire that all participate in the divine love, now and in eternity. But most importantly God reveals the intimacy of the divine self. God is the one who creates all that exists, liberates, chooses and cares, loves with merciful love, accompanies at all times, treats women and men as children of God, is willing to become one of us to redeem us and save us. God is the one who goes after the lost sheep, God is the one who suffers when we suffer.

When God catechizes, God gets involved in the complexity of our lives and our history, accepting the consequences of what that entails, yet with a unique sense of divine joy because God loves us.

God's mystery and designs are too big for the human mind and heart to grasp at once. God knows this. Consequently, the pedagogical process through which God becomes present to humanity is progressive: one step at a time, with patience. There are moments when there are misunderstandings and corrections to be made. Some cultures may need more time than others to discern the message of revelation. God walks with us. We must trust God's Holy Spirit.

What we learn from God has radical implications for the lives of people in every culture. In God's pedagogical project, we not only learn about the divine plan, but we also enter into a personal relationship with the God of revelation. As we participate in God's catechesis, one that ultimately introduces us to the mystery of Jesus Christ, we are saved. God's divine pedagogy is in essence a pedagogy of salvation.

A most fascinating aspect of this divine pedagogy is that the more we learn about God, the more we learn about our humanity. In the encounter with God in the everyday, rooted in its own cultural particularities, with its own hopes and anxieties, humanity discovers its own purpose and path to fulfillment.

God does not reject or ignore our cultural roots when entering into relationship with us. What we learn about God here and now, we learn as people living in well-defined cultural contexts that give us the tools and provide the spaces to discern that message as well as our response.

As Catholics in the United States, the more we learn about God, the more we learn about what it means to be human in all the cultural expressions that coexist in our nation. Such cultural diversity is what makes U.S. Catholicism a very enriching experience. The variety of musical expressions that accompany our liturgies every Sunday is simply fascinating! The architecture of many of Catholic churches leaves us in awe: How not to fall in love with the simple, yet inviting churches built by Spanish missionaries in the West? What about contemplating the beautiful churches built by German immigrants in the Midwest? The dialogue of Christianity with Native American traditions or with Asian philosophical traditions brought by immigrants, all coinciding in our own neighborhoods, create very unique possibilities for Catholic spirituality.

God enters in relationship with people rooted in specific cultural traditions, the message is received and embraced in light of these traditions, and with that knowledge we discern how to better live our human experience amidst diversity. Cultural diversity opens up a world of possibilities to being in relationship with God, others, and the world in light of our particularities.

The ultimate goal of God's pedagogical project is to give life to every aspect of our human existence: "I came so that they might have life and have it more abundantly" (John 10:10). That includes transforming the cultures in which we live as these allow the message of the gospel to take root so God's reign becomes a reality everywhere—and for everyone. As this occurs, God's pedagogy is prophetic. It shows the path and affirms the signs of life present in all cultures. Yet it also unmasks, confronts, and rejects the path and the signs of death, sin, and injustice that may be present in them.

IN THE FOOTSTEPS OF THE GREAT CATECHIST

There is much to learn from how God, the Great Catechist, engages culture through what we have identified as a divine pedagogy. Here are a few insights that catechists may want to keep in mind as we engage in catechetical initiatives in culturally diverse contexts:

1. Acknowledge and affirm that every person shares in

a particular cultural worldview that shapes how they understand reality and the way they relate with God, others, and the world.

2. When sharing the faith, use language—words, symbols, insights, actions—that people understand.

3. Catechesis is personal and intimate. Get involved in people's lives. Learn their cultural traditions; see how these can be instrumental for sharing the faith and building vibrant communities of faith. Share your own cultural traditions!

4. As you engage different cultural groups, take one step at a time. Catechesis is a journey, not an automatic process that seeks immediate outcomes. Walk with God's people.

5. Catechesis is more than merely communicating information or completing a program. It is an experience in which we are privileged to participate in people's journey of salvation.

6. People learn according to the cultural practices and traditions in which they grew up. Those same practices and traditions shape how they practice their faith.

7. Empower people of all ages who participate in catechetical experiences to affirm those aspects of culture that lead to life and allow God's reign to flourish. In turn, cultivate their prophetic voice to unmask, confront, and reject those aspects of one's particular culture that lead to death, sin, and injustice.

✸ *Questions for Dialogue and Reflection*

- What did you learn about God's divine pedagogy? How can you put this into practice as a catechist in a culturally diverse context?

- Think of a word or a concept that is unique in your culture/language that captures an important aspect of the Christian Catholic tradition. Describe this term and explain why you are drawn to it.

- Have you every learned or studied another language besides your mother tongue?

    If yes, describe how doing this expanded your horizon and opened new understandings about life and faith.

    If not, find someone who has and ask how doing this expanded horizons and opened new understandings about life and faith.

PART 2

How

Intercultural Competencies *for* Catechists

It is now time to delve into some of the practical implications of what the previous chapters have explored. Let us start with the question of competencies.

Would you board a plane if you knew that the pilot did not have experience flying one? What about undergoing heart surgery, knowing that the doctor in charge had never prepared to perform the special procedure you need? Most likely your answer is: no way! There is much at stake! I would not risk my life!

The two case scenarios are rather extreme, and my sense is that none of us would ever be in such a situation. However, they make a clear point: competence is very important.

In nearly every area of our daily experience there is an expectation that people act somewhat competently. The least we can expect is that teachers know how to teach, that firemen know how to put out fires, that drivers know how to operate a car, that cooks know how to cook, that preachers know how to deliver a good sermon, and so on.

We often aim at securing a certain level of competency for

what we do by means of formal education (i.e., degrees, certifications, licenses), professional development, and official authorization to perform an activity in a way that meets certain basic standards. There are also instances when competency is acquired through empirical experience, in response to a particular need in a given context, or through apprenticeship. Regardless of how we look at it, we want people who are competent at what they do.

Competency builds community and serves the common good. Competency helps us to move toward achieving our potential, both as individuals and as members of the different communities to which we belong. On the contrary, lack of competency can have real negative effects upon people's lives. All we have to do is read or listen to the daily news to find plenty of cases that prove the point!

IS THERE SUCH A THING AS CATECHETICAL COMPETENCE?

It may seem a bit strange to come to a conversation about catechesis and spend this much time talking about competencies. After all, the immense majority of catechists in Catholic communities in the United States are volunteers! Only a handful of catechetical leaders are hired as professional directors or coordinators of religious education. Should not the conversation about competencies apply only to these professionals, especially those who are hired?

Well, the answer to that question is yes and no.

Yes: dioceses, parishes, and schools usually have standards to hire and assess the competencies of those who serve as professional educators and directors or coordinators of religious education. It is imperative that the catechetical leaders in these positions be held accountable to the highest expectations, considering the importance of this ministry in the life of the church.

No: everyone engaged in the process of sharing the faith as part of a catechetical experience—including Christian parents and families at home—needs to have a basic level of competency. The 1997 *General Directory of Catechesis* offers a few important lights in this regard:

> No methodology, no matter how well tested, can dispense with the person of the catechist in every phase of the catechetical process. The **charism** given to him by the Spirit, a **solid spirituality** and **transparent witness of life**, constitutes the soul of every method. Only his own **human and Christian qualities** guarantee a good use of texts and other work instruments.
>
> The catechist is essentially a **mediator**. He **facilitates communication** between the people and the mystery of God, between subjects amongst themselves, as well as with the community. For this reason, his **cultural vision, social condition and lifestyle must not be obstacles to the journey of faith**. Rather, these help to create the most advantageous conditions for seeking out, welcoming and deepening the Christian message. He does not forget that belief is a fruit of grace and liberty. Thus, he ensures that his activities always draw support from **faith in the Holy Spirit** and from **prayer**. Finally, the **personal relationship of the catechist with the subject** is of crucial importance.
>
> *General Directory for Catechesis*, N. 156
> *Bold added for emphasis*

As we can see, there is a minimum level of expectations that all who embrace the calling to catechize must aim to meet. We can speak of these as desired competencies:

1. Awareness that being a catechist is a gift (*charism*) from the Holy Spirit;

2. Solid spirituality and prayer life;

3. Transparent witness of life;

4. Ability to facilitate communication;

5. Awareness about personal strengths and limitations;

6. Humble reliance on the Holy Spirit;

7. Knowledge of the subject.

If you think that you are not there yet, do not worry! You are not alone. Becoming a good catechist is a journey that takes time, commitment, and patience. But we must start at some point.

No one becomes competent about anything overnight. We learn by doing and by intentionally preparing for what we want to do. Exploring this book is already a step forward in becoming a more competent catechist! We become better every day. We draw important lessons from our mistakes. We grow as we witness others with more experience excel in the same ministry. To reflect further on how we grow as catechists, I suggest reading Dr. Carole Eipers' interesting book *Catechist 101, Wade Don't Dive: Giving New and Seasoned Catechists Confidence* (Twenty-Third Publications).

COMPETENCIES AND CULTURAL DIVERSITY

Tens of thousands of catechists in the United States are engaged in catechetical programs and initiatives in culturally diverse communities. Many more are discerning an invitation to do likewise. This often means sharing faith with Catholics of all ages who speak a language other than English at home, or grew up in a different country, or simply interpret reality using symbols and stories that were forged in a sociocultural context different from ours.

In the middle if this diversity, catechists and evangelizers often ask: Am I up to the task? Can I be an effective catechist sharing my faith in a culturally diverse environment? Am I sufficiently competent to accompany people of diverse cultural, linguistic, or racial/ethnic worldviews on their faith journey?

These are big questions. In fact, very important ones, since there is much at stake.

We can start addressing them by affirming the many competencies that we have already acquired just by going through the ups and downs of everyday life. We cultivate an incredible amount of competencies as we work, study, love, succeed, fail, engage in relationships, raise families, negotiate identities, participate in political processes, and practice our faith. Most of the time we take these competencies for granted, but if we were to make a list of what we know and are capable of doing, the list would be long—and very satisfying. Also, you would be surprised at how much of an expert you already are at dealing with questions of diversity and difference.

Many of these competencies are typically transferable from one context to another. If you are raising a child or have done so at some point in your life, it is likely that you would figure out a way to work with a group of children or young people in a catechetical program. If you have spent some time reading materials for a presentation at work or school, you should be able to take a catechetical guide and prepare a good session. If you have ever celebrated your faith in a particular community, chances are that you should not have a problem doing the same in a different community, even if that community speaks a different language or shares a different cultural worldview. People who travel on a regular basis know this.

But there are also competencies that need to be learned even if we have lived long, have many academic credentials, think that have seen it and heard it all, and possess a 100% level of self-confidence!

Being a successful heart surgeon does not make one an expert on brain surgery. Watching two decades of *Law & Order* does not qualify one to be a detective or to practice law. Having lived some time in Latin America or speaking Spanish does not mean that one fully understands the intricacies of ministering to Hispanic Catholics in the United States.

Catechesis in culturally diverse contexts involves a unique level of complexity that we should not minimize or take for granted. If we do, we may end up having a negative impact on the lives of many people. Let me highlight two instances that are rather common in diverse Catholic faith communities.

CASE 1: EVANGELIZATION OR ASSIMILATION?

Some ministerial and catechetical leaders seem overly concerned about Catholic immigrants being integrated into the larger U.S. society and assume that implementing catechetical initiatives or providing services only in English will accelerate the process. It is likely that some immigrants are ready and prepared to make some form of quick transition, but for most, the expectation of accelerated cultural assimilation is a burden.

Pushing for assimilation overlooks the fact that integrating into a new culture usually takes a lifetime. It also ignores the fact that most immigrants already master the predominant language at some level as they negotiate their way into the larger society, but to form their children in matters of faith and values, millions prefer their mother tongue. We need to remember that rejecting the language in which many immigrants and their children make meaning on a daily basis, including how they practice their faith, is often perceived as a rejection of one's culture and traditions.

The results can be devastating. Many Catholics, especially adults, choose not to return to a community where they do not see themselves fully embraced because cultural assimilation seems more important than evangelization. In the process, it is likely that they take their children along or simply do not encourage them to be actively involved in the life of their faith communities. Not taking into consideration the importance of one's language and cultural background for faith formation can also impact how families interact at home, since the older generation will have fewer commonalities to communicate effectively about their faith with the younger generations.

CASE 2: BIRDS OF A FEATHER?

As parishes become increasingly diverse in terms of culture, race/ethnicity, and language, some local churches are too quick to group people according to skin color or existing categories used to define particular groups. Many immigrants from Africa and the Caribbean are grouped in parishes serving African-American Catholic populations. Such organization tends to ignore linguistic and cultural backgrounds. Also, it ignores the rather different historical journeys of each group that coincide in the same parish largely because they share skin color.

Something similar happens when U.S. Hispanics are treated as a homogeneous group. In some ecclesial contexts—including offices of religious education at the diocesan and parish level—there exists the assumption that all Hispanics understand one another and share the same needs. This attitude ignores crucial linguistic differences, as in the case of many Hispanics who do not speak Spanish, like the millions born in the U.S. whose families have been in the country for many generations and are only English-speaking; or the tens of thousands of immigrants from Latin America whose first language is neither Spanish nor English but Quiche (spoken by Guatemalan indigenous groups), Tzotzil (a Mayan dialect spoken in Chiapas, Mexico), or Quechua (spoken by several indigenous groups in South America). Treating Hispanics as a homogeneous body also ignores tensions among communities that share a Hispanic background as well as the rich variety of ways of practicing the Catholic faith in the United States as Hispanics.

Because most ministry explicitly named as "Hispanic" is geared toward immigrants, the U.S.-born generation (about two-thirds of the entire Hispanic population!) often falls through wide and deep pastoral gaps, expected to live their faith either as immigrants or as fully Americanized U.S. Catholics.

Catechetical initiatives that fail to recognize the vast diversity of experiences and realities that shape the lives of Hispanic Catholics and that of other racial/ethnic groups in our country, including Euro-American, White Catholics, run the risk of becoming irrelevant.

INTERCULTURAL COMPETENCIES

Catholic pastoral and catechetical leaders in the United States have been reflecting on these dynamics for several decades. True, it is not the first time that we have contended with cultural diversity. In the past, Catholics have responded in ways that met the needs of their faith communities in light of the assumptions and possibilities of their time. While we can learn much about how U.S. Catholics dealt with cultural diversity a century ago, we live in a different time, under different circumstances, and with a distinct set of expectations about the various cultural families that constitute the church in the United States.

In the year 2011, the United States Conference of Catholic Bishops (USCCB) launched an initiative called *Building Intercultural Competencies for Ministers (BICM,* available online: http://www.usccb.org/issues-and-action/cultural-diversity/intercultural-competencies/). The main goal of this initiative is to empower Catholics in the United States to engage in the task of evangelization in a culturally diverse church with the appropriate intercultural competencies, become familiar with the potential and value of cultural diversity, and foster intercultural relationships that lead to the building of strong communities of faith.

Every Catholic catechetical leader, catechist, and pastoral agent in our country should ideally participate in training for intercultural competencies.

The Catholic bishops of the United States define intercultural competence in the following way: "Intercultural competence is the capacity to communicate, relate, and work across cultural boundaries. It involves developing capacity in three areas: knowledge, skills, and attitudes."

Let us say a few words about each area in connection to catechesis:

KNOWLEDGE INVOLVES...

Knowledge of more than one perspective on things. Keep in mind the old saying that "one size does not fit all." The presence of multiple cultural groups in our faith communities provides us with the opportunity of hearing interesting stories, learning about symbols and rituals that give life to people in different parts of the world or our own region. They can serve as a starting point for catechesis, a way to illustrate how the Christian tradition becomes life in different communities, and ways to demonstrate how people are practicing their faith.

Knowledge of different interpretations of the same cultural reality. Catechists must be attentive to how people from different cultures do things and make meaning. One good example is to be attentive to how people form family and the role of the family in passing on the faith. In many community-oriented cultures, grandparents and relatives, and not just the parents, play a major role in passing on the faith. These interpretations of reality often influence how people learn and share their religious traditions.

Knowledge of general dynamics of intercultural communication. Catechesis is ultimately an experience of encounter. It is an encounter between God and the community of believers. In this encounter, God, through the Holy Spirit, makes sure that the community understands the language of revelation and finds many ways to communicate. It is no accident that the gospel continues to grow roots in nearly every culture throughout the world. Catechesis is also an encounter among people journeying on many cultural and linguistic pathways. When these people coincide in a faith community, catechists must excel in learning patterns of communication across cultures. We need to find out how people speak, what words and gestures mean to them, and how they prefer to learn. Intercultural communication requires that as catechists we learn what to say and how to say it.

Knowledge of more than one's first language. In thousands of parishes of the United States Catholicism is a de facto bilingual experience. Learning a second language is not only an exciting adventure that sets you on the path to exploring new cultural worlds, but also a way to affirming the multiple ways in which the sacred act of communication takes place in our midst. A bilingual or multilingual catechist is a bridge, a mediator, among communities. Being bilingual opens the doors for catechists to engage entire families and connect with the ways in which they celebrate the same Catholic faith that we all profess.

SKILLS ENTAIL...

Ability to empathize. People who coincide in the catechetical experience, including the catechist, come with different experiences. We bring our hopes and anxieties, our struggles and successes, our stories and doubts. These realities are generally shaped by the cultures and circumstances that shape our lives. The catechist's main responsibility is to share the Good News, with words and actions, while exercising loving attentiveness and generous accompaniment. It is possible that we may not fully understand the complexity of people's lives or that we may be puzzled by certain situations. Yet being present and remaining open to being an instrument of God's divine presence is a good first step in the catechetical experience.

Ability to tolerate ambiguity. Catechizing in the context of cultural diversity will likely place us in situations in which opinions and perspectives collide. Ambiguity makes people uncomfortable, yet it is a part of life. Catechists need to learn how to negotiate through ambiguous situations that emerge when different cultural groups coincide: what aspects of the tradition get emphasized at any given moment? What languages do we use to share and celebrate the faith? What role should cultural particularities play in developing catechetical materials? Radical positioning may not be the most appropriate way to deal with these questions. Very often a both/and approach leads to good community building.

Ability to adapt communication and behavior. In the context of cultural diversity, it is likely that we become more sensitive to the particularities and differences of the groups that we deem "diverse." We notice linguistic patterns, ways of behaving, preferred practices and rituals, modes of relating, etc. But such sensitivity does not go only in one direction. When we see others as different, we usually do so by comparing ourselves to them. Thus, in the process, we are naming our own particularities. This is a great opportunity for catechists to do this more intentionally in order to adjust behavior and attitudes when necessary to better relate to Catholics with a different cultural background. Adjusting communication and behavior help us to grow in awareness about our own biases.

ATTITUDES INCLUDE...
Openness to others and other cultures. Considering that cultural diversity is a defining characteristic of Catholicism in the United States, it would be unrealistic and rather irresponsible to ignore others who do not share our same cultural, linguistic, or racial/ethnic background. Whether the predominant group is Hispanic, or Euro-American, or African American in any particular faith community, catechists need to cultivate an attitude of openness toward all who constitute the church in their corner of the world. Openness to others and other cultures is an invitation to contemplate the mystery of God available in the many ways that cultures mediate it.

Wanting to learn and engage other cultures. Openness is only the first step. Once catechists open our hearts and minds to the richness of cultural diversity and how God is experienced in such a context, we are invited to learn more. Cultures are worlds of meaning that reveal something fresh and exciting about humanity. Knowing that a Catholic group comes from Africa or Asia or Australia or Latin America should motivate catechists to want to learn more about these people's history and cultural traditions.

Of course, being an anthropologist is not a requirement to be a catechist! Yet allow yourself to be curious; learn and engage other cultures to be a better Catholic. Let's not forget that the word *catholic* in essence evokes the idea of universality.

Understanding intercultural interaction as a way of life, not a problem to be solved. We are in this together: Catholics from different cultures, speaking different languages, drawing from a large variety of traditions, and with distinct ways of interpreting life. We all coincide in our Catholic parishes, groups, and schools in the United States with the purpose of building God's reign here and now.

There is no doubt that a diversity of perspectives and experiences challenges how we catechize and how we organize our catechetical initiatives. Cultural diversity often thrusts us out of our comfort zone calling for the best of our creativity. Far from being a problem to be solved, cultural diversity is a way of life, a way of being church here and now. Cultural diversity is an opportunity for catechists to share the Good News in many possible ways, to address realities that often get ignored when we gloss over issues of culture or race, to appreciate the complexity of human experience, and to build faith communities that embody the mark of Catholicity in a real, tangible way.

Mindfulness. Sharing the Good News in a culturally diverse church is an invitation to mind. Yes, mind how we honor the cultural realities that shape people's lives in their present existence; mind the obstacles and biases that prevent us from being an authentically welcoming church; mind the many ways in which God is experienced in our midst.

❀ *Questions for Dialogue and Reflection*

- Name a couple of experiences or situations in your life that you think have prepared you to be a good catechist.

- What would you say is your most obvious limitation in serving as a catechist in a culturally diverse context? Name the competencies that you think will help you to overcome such limitation.

- What skills have you cultivated to engage cultural diversity with a positive attitude?

- Briefly share a story about a time when you were exposed to a person or a group that you considered culturally different and learned something important about *yourself* (2 to 3 minutes).

- What can your parish/diocese/school/group do to help you develop intercultural competencies? With whom should you speak about this?

Dos *and* Don'ts *about* Culture

There are few things that cause more joy in the heart of a catechist than the opportunity to share the faith with passion and conviction. To share one's faith through catechesis is to be part of someone's journey of encounter with God, others, and the world. Ultimately, it is an opportunity to accompany fellow Christians on their path toward fullness and holiness. There is something sacred about teaching catechesis, and we want to do it well.

It is possible that some catechists feel that teaching the faith in a culturally diverse context is like walking through a minefield: if they say the wrong word or do the wrong thing, then a mine will explode and the entire experience will be over. Many see themselves unprepared to engage Catholics from cultural and linguistic backgrounds different from their own, and thus prefer to defer this important ministry to catechists with more expertise, usually from the communities where those to be catechized come from. I have met catechists who decide not to teach children or young people or adults from a different racial/ethnic group to avoid misunderstandings.

I have also met very well-intentioned catechists who claim to have a position of "cultural neutrality" when teaching the faith, focusing exclusively on the content of the faith.

All these scenarios are plausible and rather common in culturally diverse communities. However, it is healthy to separate reasonable concerns from some excessive caution that may stifle the catechetical process:

- Sharing faith certainly presupposes that catechists will eventually develop some competencies that help them address questions of cultural and linguistic diversity. Yet the process is far from being a minefield! It is fine to make mistakes, to acknowledge that we do not know the meaning of a symbol or tradition from a given culture, and to mispronounce words in a different language.

- While it is always good to have catechists with the skills to address cultural and linguistic differences and to empower those that have first-hand knowledge of a particular cultural group because they belong to it, all catechists should remain open to sharing the Good News with everyone. Catechesis is about witnessing what we have experienced. The language of love, kindness, and caring is ultimately the most effective medium for sharing one's faith. Jesus modeled this for us.

- Not to catechize people from a different culture or whose first language is different from ours for fear of misunderstandings may rob us of the opportunity to learn from their rich experiences of faith. As long as we remain open to being corrected and to respectfully acknowledging that there are different ways of living our relationship with God through Jesus Christ, a misunderstanding should be nothing but an opportunity to grow in love for our sisters and brothers.

- Strictly speaking, "cultural neutrality" is an illusion. We all speak out of a cultural framework. We all use the words, concepts, and symbols that we learned within a particular cultural context. If I am Euro-American, White, I see the world and practice my faith as such. And I should be proud of it. If I am African American, I see the world and practice my faith as such. And I should be proud of it. To pretend that a person can leave one's culture behind while sharing one's faith can reduce catechesis to a cold, impersonal process of sharing data. Catechesis is much more than that! Catechesis is a personal and warm exercise of sharing one's experience of faith, of giving witness of what God has done in our lives, of echoing the beauty of the Christian tradition that has given life to countless people throughout history.

Catechists need to be careful not to turn culture into a taboo when sharing their faith in culturally diverse contexts. The following Dos and Don'ts serve as practical suggestions to prepare ourselves to better engage questions of culture in our faith communities.

Five Dos

1. DO RESPECT THE CULTURAL EXPRESSIONS THROUGH WHICH PEOPLE PRACTICE THEIR FAITH.

Catholics in the United States practice and celebrate their faith in a rich variety of ways. Many of those ways are shaped by cultural traditions that have evolved in our own communities; others arrived with the millions of immigrants who give life to our faith communities.

Some cultural expressions may seem at odds with our aesthetic sensibilities. For instance, many Hispanic and Asian Catholics are drawn to images of Jesus that more explicitly evoke his *suffering* on the cross. Some Catholics prefer the organ for sacred music—others prefer guitars and drums. Some Catholics are very reserved during worship; others are more outspoken and more emotionally expressive.

Each particular cultural manifestation that helps Catholics express their faith connects to something much bigger, usually family or community or worldview. Our role as catechists is not to categorize some as "better" or "more acceptable" than others. All these expressions are starting points to enter more deeply into the mystery of God. When such expressions obviously lead away from God, then it is a responsibility of the catechist to discern with the community and offer alternatives.

2. DO LEARN ABOUT WHAT PARTICULAR CULTURAL GROUPS TREASURE AS THEIR OWN AS THEY DEFINE THEIR IDENTITY.

There is something sacred about how people define their communal identity. Even though we all live in the larger context of the United States of America, it is very likely that a Native-American Catholic group would highlight certain cultural traits that are unique to their identity. In turn, a group of Euro-American, White Catholics would probably highlight different ones.

Some Catholics in the United States would point to their history of struggles as a defining characteristic of their identity. One cannot ignore, for instance, that many of our African-American Catholic sisters and brothers trace a direct line to ancestors who were slaves. Other Catholics would highlight major accomplishments as their parents and grandparents settled and grew strong roots in this nation. Others are particularly sensitive to migratory experiences and stories because they or their most immediate relatives are immigrants.

Catechists should take the time to learn about the particular journeys of the communities they are serving. Each story is a glimpse of how God becomes present in our shared history.

3. DO LISTEN TO THE STORIES THAT CARRY DREAMS, HOPES, CONCERNS, AND HOW PEOPLE FROM DIFFERENT CULTURES INTERPRET THE WORLD.

Every culture has a set of foundational stories that carry dreams, hopes, concerns, and worldviews. In those stories we encounter heroes, unknown places to go, challenges to overcome, and battles that defined the destiny of entire nations. These stories inspire us and are passed on from generation to generation as reminders of who we are as a community.

Very often these stories have religious undertones: God led the people to freedom...God chose a particular community to reveal something to the world...divine signs were given to confirm that what was happening was meant by God's wisdom...a prophecy was fulfilled.

Many of those foundational stories name specifically how Catholics see God accompanying them in the United States. Some narratives tell the saga of Catholic immigrants fleeing hardship or persecution to recreate lives and whole communities in a new land. There are narratives that point to the deep faith of the people and the conviction that God has a special love for those who struggle the most. A case in point is the story of the apparitions of Our Lady of Guadalupe, especially treasured by Hispanic Catholics. Biblical narratives frequently acquire renewed meaning when read by U.S. Catholics in light of their particular experience: the Exodus, the crossing of the desert, the Passion, Pentecost, etc.

Be attentive to people's stories. Listen carefully. Link them to the larger Christian story.

4. DO PAY ATTENTION TO HOW PEOPLE FROM DIFFERENT CULTURES TEACH AND LEARN.

Most of the great minds reflecting about education agree that this is a relational process. Yes, there is information to be memorized and processed, texts that need to be studied, and goals to be achieved through education. Nonetheless, most of what stays in our minds and hearts is usually that which we learn by being in relationship with others, that which helps us to build relationships.

Cultures tend to affirm particular ways of teaching and learning that ultimately help them to build community. In doing so, some privilege the role of the elders and authorities while others put more emphasis on the individual person as a critical learner. Some invest significantly in technical skills while others are more concerned about giving people skills to wrestle with the big questions of life. Not one size fits all. Each emphasis has its own strengths and weaknesses.

These ways of teaching and learning also influence how people share faith. The educational system in the United States, for instance, tends to favor the grade-school structure, critical thinking methods, the use of written texts, and the constant engagement of technology. Catechesis in thousands of parishes follows those patterns. Catechists need to keep in mind, however, that there are many Catholics, immigrants and U.S.-born, who prefer to learn sharing their faith in small communities, or through storytelling, or using popular Catholicism, or participating actively in the liturgy, or praying at home, among other practices, or through a combination of all these. The more we know about the cultural background of Catholics in our communities, the more familiar we will become with these ways of teaching and learning.

5. DO PRAY AND CELEBRATE WITH CATHOLICS FROM DIFFERENT CULTURAL BACKGROUNDS.

Despite our cultural or linguistic differences, in the celebration of the Eucharist and the rest of the sacraments we uniquely experience being in communion with God and with one another. It is possible that some may imagine that the church as an institution would impose one specific way of celebrating the liturgy to preserve that unity—say, one language or one type of music or one rigid set of movements. But the wisdom of the Christian tradition over the centuries reminds us that communion is not tantamount to cultural homogeneity!

The *Catechism of the Catholic Church* affirms: "It is fitting that liturgical celebration tends to express itself in the culture of the people where the Church finds herself, though without being submissive to it. Moreover, the liturgy itself generates cultures and shapes them" (N. 1207). This conviction echoes the vision of the Second Vatican Council: "Even in the liturgy, the Church has no wish to impose a rigid uniformity in matters which do not implicate the faith or the good of the whole community; rather does she respect and foster the genius and talents of the various races and peoples" (Constitution on the Sacred Liturgy, N. 37).

There is much to learn from the many ways and languages in which Catholics from different cultures celebrate the liturgy in the United States. Allow yourself as a catechist to give praise to God by participating in culturally diverse liturgical celebrations, contemplate the many ways in which faith and culture come together, discover how different cultures interpret and celebrate the mystery of God! Your perspective as a catechist and as a fellow sojourner in the Catholic faith will be profoundly transformed.

Five Don'ts

1. DON'T ACT AS IF ONLY "OTHERS" HAVE A CULTURE.

On occasion, we may refer to people from other groups, especially those who do not look or speak like us, as "people who have a culture." The irony is that in doing so we fail to acknowledge that we also have one! This can happen when we fall into the trap of reducing culture to merely race or ethnicity or language. It can also happen when we think that culture is mainly defined by external expressions like dress, food, or music that are different from those with which we are familiar.

But as we saw earlier, culture is much more than external expressions. Culture is a way of life, a matrix within which we live and interpret the world, both individually and communally. From this perspective, everyone has a culture! We may certainly learn new cultures and transition from one to another. Yet, it is humanly impossible to live outside a particular culture.

Culture deeply shapes how we understand the mystery of God, our prayer life, the way we learn the faith, and the way we share it with others. A good exercise that all catechists need to do is to name how particular cultural perspectives shape our personal experience. In doing this we will grow in humility.

2. DON'T ASSUME THAT ALL CULTURES ARE THE SAME.

One of the most beautiful aspects about the human experience is that it can be expressed in many ways. How people live their humanity, make meaning, raise families, care for one another, share knowledge, and build society is normally informed by specific cultural frameworks that shape our lives. When we take the time to learn and appreciate how the miracle of being human is expressed in the context of diverse cultures, we cannot but be awestruck at the many ways in which humanity can flourish.

It is true that cultures share many elements in common.

There are some cultures that are very similar in the way they approach family life and religious practice. In the United States of America, Hispanic Catholics find striking commonalities with Asian Catholics and Catholics of African descent. Even though some cultures may seem significantly different because of language or geographical distances, when their members live in the same place they soon realize that their understanding of the world or how they relate to God has many similarities.

But it would be naïve for catechists and evangelizers to assume that similarities automatically blur cultural differences. We all are children of our particular cultures, and we act in the world as women and men shaped by such cultural realities.

Catholics in the United States have a very particular way of living our faith and interpreting the larger reality, precisely because of our own cultural location. Sometimes we do not know how American we are until we travel outside the country or are exposed to immigrants from other parts of the world. Yes, as Catholics in the United States we are very American in the broad sense of the word. This is our culture, one constituted by many cultural influences. In fact, it is accurate to say that there are many ways of being American Catholics, and each has much to contribute to building the church and the larger U.S. society.

3. DON'T BUY INTO THE IDEA THAT ONE CULTURE IS "BETTER" THAN ANOTHER FOR SHARING THE FAITH.

The Judeo-Christian tradition introduces us to God, whose merciful love and revelation message is for all. The gift of salvation that we receive in the person of Jesus Christ is for everyone. This clearly points to the universal character of Christianity. All women and men, without exception, are called to experience God's salvific love.

But when God enters in relationship with humanity in history, God does it in very particular ways. As we saw earlier, Jesus of Nazareth, the Word made flesh, was born, lived, and died as a Jew. His life was profoundly shaped by the Jewish culture of his time.

While there is much to value about the Jewish culture in biblical times, and catechists do well to become familiar with the social and cultural dynamics that shaped the life of Jesus and the first Christian disciples, one does not have to become culturally Jewish to be a faithful Christian.

For many centuries Christianity was associated with European cultures, yet one does not have to become culturally European to be a faithful Christian. Today, about half of all Catholics in the United States are Hispanic, yet one does not have to become culturally Hispanic to be a faithful U.S. Catholic. If at some point someone thinks or acts otherwise, then such inversion of values needs to be denounced since it may lead into the "idolatry of culture."

From the very beginning Christians, guided by God's Holy Spirit, have brought the message of the gospel into countless cultures and allowed it to grow roots in dialogue with them. Catholics often speak of this process as "inculturation."

As the message of the gospel grows in the heart of every culture, cultures are transformed. The gospel affirms the elements of truth and goodness in each culture and rejects those elements that embody sin and prevent people from flourishing according to their dignity as children of God. In that process, the transformed elements of culture offer glimpses of what God's reign can be.

But there is no culture that can claim to be perfectly Christian or the best medium to channel the gospel! Catechists should become experts in identifying the best ways in which each culture can mediate the richness of the gospel and cultivate those ways. When sharing the faith in a culturally diverse context or community, much of our work consists in determining the potential of particular cultural expressions to nurture Christian identity. More often than not, we are going to encounter many! Some of these are perhaps different from our regular cultural standards. Some will challenge us but in turn will open our horizons. Allow yourself to be surprised!

4. DON'T UNDERESTIMATE THE CONSEQUENCES OF CULTURAL BIASES.

During colonial times, many Catholic missionaries, largely from Spain, were remarkably zealous about preaching the gospel and establishing faith communities in Latin America and the Caribbean. They were successful in many aspects, but one in which they failed notably was the cultivation of native clergy and local leaders. For centuries, most of the clergy and women religious in these parts of the world came from Spain. When things became difficult, these leaders would return to Spain or go somewhere else and leave communities without appropriate pastoral care. Prejudice against natives, especially those with indigenous, mixed race, and Black roots, led many to assume that men from these communities would not make good priests. Many were never accepted in seminaries. Cultural and racial biases ran deep. Thank God much of that has changed. However, Latin America was not the only case. Something similar happened in Asia, Africa, and even in the United States of America!

This brief case study illustrates two realities. On the one hand, it brings our attention to the fact we all likely have preconceived ideas about how people can live their Christian discipleship and exercise leadership in our faith communities. Such preconceived ideas are deeply rooted in our own cultural expectations. In the United States, for instance, the predominant model of ministerial leadership often presupposes strong academic credentials (i.e., college degrees) and some level of professionalization on the part of an individual. This model sometimes contrasts with models espoused by some immigrant communities, which favor communal formation, shared leadership, and some form of "charismatic" affirmation — read "charismatic" as Spirit-led initiative confirmed by the prayer and support of the particular faith community. Both models draw from very specific cultural wells. Both have much to offer to how Catholics live and practice our identity as missionary disciples in a culturally diverse church.

On the other hand, we learn about the negative consequences that our own cultural biases can have. Sometimes we may feel that practices that reveal explicit cultural preferences (e.g., popular Catholicism, ways of praying, ways of expressing oneself physically in the liturgy, etc.) do not have room in our faith communities because they are "new" or "different" or "disrupting." They challenge the way we have always done things. It is possible that we think that some Catholics will not be effective catechizing or evangelizing in our community because they are "too different" from us. Such attitudes can easily end up hindering our entire efforts to share the gospel and build communities of faith where everyone experiences the love of God through Jesus Christ.

Regardless of the ethnic, racial, or cultural group with which we self-identify, one good way of balancing those attitudes is to imagine ourselves on the other side of the equation as "cultural minorities." How would we react if someone told us: "The way you practice your faith as a *'(racial/ethnic/cultural group)'* Catholic is too novel, different, and rather disruptive. Please change and do it in a different way so you can fit in our community." Or, "Even though you are Catholic, I think that you would not be an effective catechist or evangelizer in our community because you are 'too different' from us, speak differently, and share cultural values that we don't understand." When cultural, racial, and ethnic biases predominate, either in church or in the larger society, everyone loses.

5. DON'T IGNORE THE LIMITATIONS OF CULTURE.

Cultures do not exist in the abstract. Cultures are matrices within which flesh-and-blood people live, making sense of their own realities, building relationships, transforming the world, and journeying toward some form of fulfillment. Cultures are very human. And as human realities, cultures have limitations.

As the gospel enters in dialogue with culture and grows its roots affirming the elements of life and grace in it, Christians soon discover that there are elements of sin and evil in every culture that prevent the reign of God from flourishing in our midst. Sometimes these elements are so ingrained in a particular culture that they may pass for normal or legal, perhaps desirable. Examples abound. Christians need to be attentive to practices, expressions, and convictions that privilege deceit, that marginalize and exclude people, especially the most vulnerable, and that tolerate injustice, threaten life, and promote materialism and a life without God, etc.

As ministers of the Word, catechists are uniquely positioned to raise our prophetic voices with the rest of the Christian community to name the limitations of our cultures and denounce those elements that are clearly against the gospel. To do this, catechists must draw from the rich treasure of the Christian Tradition, particularly the Scriptures and the best of Catholic Social Teaching as we share the faith with the next generations. But most important, in embracing the commitment to witnessing and practicing the faith that we teach, catechists emerge as "cultural critics," women and men who possess the wisdom to affirm the best and name the limitations of culture, starting with our own.

✹ *Questions for Dialogue and Reflection*

- What was the "Do" in this chapter that resonated most with you, and why?

- What was the "Don't" in this chapter that resonated most with you, and why?

- Share a story, an anecdote, or a practice that you learned from someone who is not from your own cultural/racial or linguistic background that has helped you to become a better Catholic.

- What are some of the cultural biases that you have encountered in your faith community and how do they affect how catechesis and ministry are done?

- What should catechists in your parish, school, or faith community do to discuss more openly questions related to racism and cultural biases, both as a group and with the people they teach?

Ten Tips *to* Organize (or Reorganize) Catechetical Programs *in* Culturally Diverse Contexts

Christians have been engaged in the process of sharing the faith for two millennia. We have learned a lot in the process. From the very beginning, Christian missionaries, teachers, preachers, and catechists realized that if the message of the gospel was to touch people's lives, the way in which that message was communicated needed to be adapted to the particular circumstances in which people lived. Catechesis must take into consideration the cultural realities that shape people's lives, how they make meaning, and their ways of knowing reality. St. Thomas Aquinas wisely noted that "whatever is received is received according to the mode of the receiver."

Organizing a catechetical program is a major task in itself! There are many practical aspects that need to be considered, including training catechists, selecting materials, scheduling, and reserving spaces where the catechetical experience will take place. Thinking about diversity, particularly issues of culture, language, and race/ethnicity, adds another layer of complexity to the planning process.

In culturally diverse contexts, however, catechists need to engage culture as a priority if we want to be responsible to those circumstances and experiences that shape people's lives in the everyday. If catechesis fails to address and engage the cultural dynamics that mediate how God becomes present in the here and now of our existence, we run the risk of running initiatives that are ultimately irrelevant and disconnected from people's everyday existence.

It is possible that you are in a faith community or a school setting where catechesis follows a model that has been in place for a long while and may have worked well in the past. Perhaps such a model was established at a time when catechetical leaders did not have to worry about different cultural and linguistic groups sharing the faith in the same space. However, if that community or school setting is experiencing an influx of culturally diverse groups, then catechesis needs to be reorganized.

The following are ten practical tips to organize (or reorganize) catechetical programs in culturally diverse contexts that catechists and catechetical leaders can implement with some level of intentionality. The tips are not cold and unengaged suggestions that call for catechists to go behind a desk to envision a master plan in their minds with the hope that it will work for everyone. On the contrary, they are rooted in the conviction that planning a catechetical initiative is a deeply relational experience.

Just as in politics, all catechesis is local! The following tips are not rigid formulas but general recommendations that aim at creating an environment for creative conversations about catechesis and cultural diversity.

As you go through these tips, my hope is that at the end you can say: "I can do that"!

1. PRAY FOR WISDOM TO KNOW WHAT TO DO.

Prayer is always a good way to start the discernment about what needs to be done to organize a catechetical program. After all, it is the Holy Spirit who will guide the process, prepare and move the hearts of those who will be involved, inspire catechists, and ensure that the gifts that the baptized receive will bear fruit for the good of the entire community.

Two passages come to mind about a community of Christian disciples praying before engaging in catechesis and evangelization in the context of diversity. Both passages come from the Acts of the Apostles.

The first passage is in Acts, chapter 2. The disciples had gathered to pray and discern about what to do next after the Ascension. They most likely knew that the task of announcing the Good News to the many people living in Jerusalem would be titanic. Fear and uncertainty may have entered their hearts. On the day of Pentecost, they received the Holy Spirit: "they were all filled with the Holy Spirit and began to speak in different tongues, as the Spirit enabled them to proclaim" (Acts 2:4). With the Spirit in their hearts, they knew what to do and how to do it with a very diverse population.

Later on in the book of Acts, this time in chapter 10, Peter discerns about the idea of baptizing Cornelius, a Roman soldier, a Gentile. While in prayer, he receives assurance of God's plans. Peter comes to the house of Cornelius and asserts, "I see that God shows no partiality. Rather, in every nation whoever fears him and acts uprightly is acceptable to him" (Acts 10:34–35). The Spirit comes upon Cornelius and those in his house; then all are baptized. This passage is a reminder of the universality of salvation. Diversity is not an obstacle to experience the richness of God's merciful love.

When in doubt about what to do, pray. God will show the way.

2. KNOW WELL YOUR COMMUNITY AND THE PEOPLE YOU WILL MEET
IN THE CATECHETICAL EXPERIENCE.

It could be tempting for some catechists to assume that as long as one "stays on topic," focused primarily on content and texts like a catechism or a catechetical guide, there is no need to get too personal or too concerned about cultural or personal realities.

However, a Catholic understanding of catechesis suggests otherwise. Catechesis is deeply personal. It intentionally engages our everyday experience, takes culture seriously, and is very concerned about how we bring our faith into practice. It could not get more personal than that.

Every person and every group has a story. Take the time to learn about the different cultural and linguistic groups in your faith community. Here are three ways to get to know more about them:

a. Read a short history about each particular group. If they are immigrants or children of immigrants, learn about their history of migration. You can go to a library or search online.

b. Meet two or three people from those communities, ideally of different ages, and ask them to share some stories. You can ask these five questions in a short conversation:
   - *Who are you? Say a little about what you do.*
   - *Can you share something about the place where you grew up?*
   - *What do you appreciate most about the cultural/ethnic/*

> *linguistic community to which you belong?*
> - *What is one of the religious traditions you like most in your community?*
> - *In what ways do you feel that you belong to this parish (or school or group)?*

c. If these communities celebrate the Eucharist in a language different from yours, or perhaps another liturgical moment or ritual, make the time to attend. Observe...listen...contemplate...allow yourself to be drawn into the experience.

Take some notes, and discuss them with your fellow catechists, friends, and family.

3. LISTEN CAREFULLY TO DIFFERENT VOICES.

Take advantage of the wisdom about sharing faith that already exists in each of the cultural groups in your community. Inquire about how parents in various cultural groups pass on the faith to their children. Ask about how families pray at home. Identify if parents and relatives have any struggles accompanying the young in the process of sharing the faith.

Very often, catechetical and pastoral leaders plan entire catechetical programs based on their experience, instinct, or professional expertise, practically without consulting those groups in the community that will be most impacted by their decisions. Often, groups that fall under the narrow categories of "minorities" or "cultural" are left out of processes of consultation.

Pastors, catechetical leaders, and school administrators frequently make executive decisions about catechetical materials without having a conversation about how such materials incorporate the experience of the various cultural groups in a community. Allegiance to a publisher may not be enough when selecting materials for bilingual catechesis or faith formation initiatives that form people to live and practice their faith in a diverse church and society.

At the level of logistics, inquire about the best times to hold catechetical meetings. Many communities assume that weekends and evenings are among the best timeframes to do that. Yet, in communities with large number of immigrants, the timeframes for meetings may be different. Multicultural communities in urban and busy settings may not have the flexibility of the suburban context.

One common concern in multilingual communities is the language of catechesis. Opinions about this vary from community to community. Some catechists insist on a "one-language-only" approach for catechesis. Some immigrants want to use catechesis as a moment to teach and cultivate language and cultural traditions. Some communities have catechesis in two, three, or even more languages. In catechetical programs for children and youth whose parents are immigrants, it is common to discover that parents do not always agree with their children about the best language to use when teaching the faith to their young ones.

Based on a couple of decades of experience and having engaged numerous catechetical leaders in conversation in dozens of dioceses, here is my threefold rule of thumb:

1. honor the core purpose of catechesis, namely to facilitate a transforming encounter with the Good News of Jesus Christ and the richness of the Christian tradition;

2. integrate as many cultural and linguistic elements as possible that facilitate the first part of this rule while ensuring that those elements do not overshadow the core purpose of the catechetical experience; and

3. offer catechesis in the language that *the one being catechized* is most comfortable. If this means offering catechesis in several languages, the faith community should find a way to do so. The needs will vary from community of community.

One last note about language: it is commonplace that many children born in the United States who are being raised by immigrant parents (or relatives) and speak a different language at home prefer to be catechized in English. This tends to be the language used for most affairs outside their homes. It is a good practice for catechists to foster moments of encounter between these children and their families through meetings, retreats, and even catechetical sessions in the language of the immigrant adults. This practice involves the members of the household in the catechetical experience and provides an opportunity to foster family catechesis. It also helps to address the perception that language differences are irreconcilable when sharing faith.

Consult with leaders at the diocesan, regional, or national level who have expertise on these matters. They most likely are familiar with good practices that can help your catechetical program in a culturally diverse context thrive.

4. FORM A GROUP OF ADVISORS.

Not long ago many Catholic parishes had religious education committees that helped pastors and directors of catechetical programs to monitor initiatives related to faith formation and support catechetical leaders. Committees still exist in some parishes, though, unfortunately, the practice is not as widespread as it used to be.

Organizing a catechetical program in a context shaped by cultural diversity requires a lot of energy, insight, and consultation. The creation of a local advisory committee to provide input on catechetical matters in these contexts would be very beneficial. This committee should bring together on a regular basis the major pastoral stakeholders in the community and representatives of the cultural, linguistic, and racial/ethnic groups that coexist in the parish. It would be helpful to invite persons with some expertise in pedagogy, multicultural education, and curriculum development. The committee can help to envision a solid catechetical program, support its leaders, and train catechists. It can also assess how effective the program is in meeting the faith formation needs of all cultural groups in the community.

5. PROCURE REGULAR TRAINING FOR CATECHETICAL LEADERS AND CATECHISTS ON TOPICS RELATED TO INTERCULTURAL COMPETENCIES.

Catechists draw from the best of our experiences and instincts to share the faith with Catholics of different ages. Sometimes, past experience and instinct are not enough to make us effective educators in the faith; hence the need for some regular training about the nuts and bolts of catechesis. Also, basic experience and instinct may not suffice when addressing matters related to racial/ethnic, cultural, and linguistic diversity. There is much at stake when we share the faith. Besides the importance of accompanying people on their journey of faith, catechesis plays a major role in preparing Catholics to build communities that are faithful and inclusive.

All catechetical leaders and catechists should learn and cultivate the appropriate intercultural competencies to serve in the church in the United States. This applies more immediately to those serving in the thousands of Catholic parishes in the country that have multiple cultural, linguistic, and racial/ethnic communities; however, every Catholic catechist should learn these competencies. The Catholic bishops of the United

States define intercultural competence as "the capacity to communicate, relate, and work across cultural boundaries. It involves developing capacity in three areas: knowledge, skills, and attitudes." Chapter 5 in this book provides important details about this important topic.

As catechists in our Catholic faith communities and educational institutions become more interculturally competent, they bring the learned knowledge, skills, and attitudes to bear upon the many ways they serve diverse groups. Nonetheless, catechists who are interculturally competent are uniquely positioned to help all Catholics in parishes and schools, particularly the predominant groups, to understand the complexity of being culturally diverse communities. This includes incorporating in faith-formation sessions, according to the level of those being catechized, discussions about causes of mass migration, poverty, working conditions that shape the lives of immigrants, social biases (e.g., racism), and the challenges of living in a pluralistic society.

6. RECRUIT, PREPARE, AND EMPOWER CATECHETICAL LEADERS AND CATECHISTS FROM THE CULTURAL GROUPS YOU ARE SERVING.

The best catechists come from the faith community itself. These are women and men of various ages who know the local dynamics of the community, are familiar with the families and the neighborhood, worship with them, and can make important connections between catechesis and the lives of those being catechized.

In culturally diverse communities catechizing children, youth, and adults from different cultural, linguistic, and racial/ethnic groups, it is important to identify catechists who come from those particular groups. They embody natural intercultural competencies that make important connections possible.

Young people who are bilingual and bicultural are incredible resources. Do not hesitate to engage them! This can also be an opportunity to plant in their hearts the idea of discerning a vocation to permanent service in the church.

Sometimes parishes or schools need catechists who lead catechetical sessions in a language other than English. There is no need to learn a new language every time these situations emerge. If you have done your homework engaging the different cultural groups, then you should be able to identify, train, and cultivate a catechist who can do this.

Make sure that catechists from all backgrounds in your community share their faith across cultural and linguistic boundaries with as many Catholics as possible. Being an Asian catechist does not mean that one can only catechize Asian Catholics. Mutual exposure across cultures allows for a rich interchange of experiences, stories and multiple ways of bringing to life the richness of our Catholic faith.

Even though U.S. Catholics are incredibly diverse, the vast majority of directors of religious education in the United States at the parish, diocesan, and school levels are Euro-American, White. Engaging catechists from different cultural backgrounds is also a unique opportunity to cultivate a new generation of catechetical leaders that reflects the diversity of our faith communities at the grassroots level.

7. IDENTIFY RESOURCES THAT TAKE CULTURAL DIVERSITY SERIOUSLY (E.G., GUIDES, VIDEOS, BOOKS, WEBSITES).

In recent years, publishing companies and organizations developing catechetical materials have intensified their efforts to integrate more elements from different cultural perspectives into their resources. There are many bilingual catechetical guides available. Images and pictures in printed and digital materials tend to portray Catholics from different racial/ethnic and cultural backgrounds practicing their faith. It is more common to see practices, rituals, and symbols from different cultural groups being used to illustrate important points of the Catholic faith.

When choosing catechetical materials in culturally diverse contexts, make sure to consider how these materials engage the culture of the particular group you hope to engage in faith formation. Yes, culture and language matter. When someone sees a resource that connects to a personal aspect of their life or their culture, the level of engagement and interest increases significantly. Do not take culture and language for granted.

Besides the regular catechetical guides, search online and visit a library or a diocesan resource center for materials that can help you communicate your message while engaging the cultural, ethnic/racial, and linguistic groups in your faith community. Develop a list of resources. Invite speakers from those particular groups to share their stories and how they practice their faith.

8. DEVELOP MODELS OF LESSON PLANNING THAT INTENTIONALLY INTEGRATE CULTURE.

While we envision the building blocks for catechetical programs in culturally diverse settings, we need to be attentive not to limit our mindfulness about culture, race/ethnicity, and language to the macro-level planning. As they say, "the proof is in the pudding."

We need to bring our commitment to seriously engaging culture to the most basic aspect of the catechetical session: lesson planning. In her very helpful book *Here's How, A Catechist's Guide: Planning and Teaching Your Catechetical Sessions* (Twenty-Third Publications), Lee Danesco invites catechists to make time to plan their lessons: "No matter the grade level, the class size, or the lesson content, every class you teach requires basic, commonsense planning. There is no escaping that chore. Planning is the pivot around which every lesson revolves" (p. 4). I definitely recommend reading her book if you wish to grow in the skill of lesson planning.

It is possible that the materials that you will be using already have some references to a particular cultural practice, story, or devotion. But it is likely that those materials have been prepared for very wide audiences and do not always connect with the experience of some of the cultural, linguistic, and racial/ethnic groups in your community. It is also possible that the engagement of culture is too broad. So here is where you can make a difference.

Let's say that you divide your class into five moments: opening prayer, reading, skits, group discussion, and closing reflection (see Lee Danesco's book, p. 24). This is just one way of organizing your time. You can adapt this structure in many other ways. As you plan your lesson, make a couple of commitments that become standard in terms of how you catechize: 1) include a prayer, reading, or story that connects directly with one or two of the cultural communities represented in your group. 2) Develop a handout (e.g., image, poem, song, story, ritual) that illustrates how a cultural group in your community brings to life and celebrates the topic of a particular catechetical session. Invite those in your group to talk about that handout at home.

I strongly invite directors of religious education and other catechetical leaders to make these suggestions standard in their programs, especially if they are serving culturally diverse communities. This should not be optional. It is likely that some catechists may not have the skill or time to easily make such integration while planning their lessons. This is where the catechetical leader comes in, training and providing resources, supporting and assessing.

Appreciation for cultural diversity does not happen by accident. It needs to be cultivated with a strong level of intentionality. The moment of lesson planning is crucial to achieve this goal.

9. PLAN TO INVOLVE FAMILIES FROM THE BEGINNING.

Church documents about catechesis consistently remind us about the importance of the family as the space where we first learn about our faith and where it is cultivated. The 1997 *General Directory for Catechesis* insists: "Parents are the primary educators in the faith. Together with them, especially in certain cultures, all members of the family play an active part in the education of the younger members" (N. 255). Though we know this, sometimes we fail to make it happen. Many parents and relatives in turn seem to be rather at ease "outsourcing" this responsibility to catechists and teachers.

Catechesis in culturally diverse contexts should take advantage of the different ways of being family in the faith community. For many immigrant families, for instance, sharing cultural practices and traditions is a deeply family-oriented experience. Passing on the faith and learning basic values is perceived as a primary responsibility of the family. Catechetical programs ought to build upon these convictions.

In the case of children of immigrants, involving the family may require using several languages beyond the one that is predominant in the community.

10. IMMERSE YOURSELF IN THE LIFE OF THE CULTURAL GROUPS THAT YOU ARE SERVING.

Although we can point to particular catechetical moments when we meet specifically to share and discuss our faith, catechesis is part of a much larger experience. As Catholics learn and discern our faith, we are constantly making connections between what happens in the catechetical moment and the rest of our lives.

All dimensions in the life of our faith communities contribute to the catechetical experience: the celebration of the liturgy and the sacraments, prayer groups, the instances in which we bring our faith to action serving those most in need, how we build one community amidst differences, our participation in public and civic life as Catholics, Bible study groups, etc. That catechetical experience is also deeply influenced by what happens in the day-to-day of our lives: at home, at work, at school, in our relationships, etc.

Catechetical leaders and catechists need to get involved in what happens in the life of the diverse groups we serve to help them make those connections. Getting involved does not mean violating boundaries but expressing care and commitment out of merciful love.

In the process of getting involved, we learn much about the realities and circumstances that shape the lives of the many people we meet in the catechetical experience. Pope Francis reminds us that getting involved is an important aspect of the evangelization process: "An evangelizing community gets involved by word and deed in people's daily lives; it bridges distances, it is willing to abase itself if necessary, and it embraces human life, touching the suffering flesh of Christ in others. Evangelizers thus take on the 'smell of the sheep'" (*The Joy of the Gospel*, N. 24). Getting involved strengthens the bonds of solidarity and prompts us to understand catechesis as a true experience of building communion in the midst of diversity.

⬢ *Questions for Dialogue and Reflection*

- What did you find most helpful for your catechetical program about the tips shared in this chapter?

- Where do you go and whom do you consult when you need resources that resonate with the cultural, racial/ethnic, or linguistic particularity of the groups in your faith community? (Make a short list that you can potentially share with others).

- What can you do in your catechetical program to empower catechists from the different cultural groups to serve in this important ministry? Propose at least five practical commitments to foster diversity.

- If your faith community or school is culturally diverse and already has a catechetical program, what elements from the above list of tips need to be implemented to strengthen that program?